HODDER AND STOUGHTON'S
PEOPLE'S LIBRARY

General Editor : Sidney Dark

HODDER & STOUGHTON'S
PEOPLE'S LIBRARY

General Editor   SIDNEY DARK.

HODDER & STOUGHTON   H&S   LIMITED, LONDON, E.C. 4

JOHN BUNYAN

BY

W. H. HUTTON, D.D.

DEAN OF WINCHESTER

H&S

HODDER AND STOUGHTON
PUBLISHERS   LONDON

TO

A LEARNED SCHOLAR

IN THE LIFE AND LITERATURE OF

THE SEVENTEENTH-CENTURY,

TO

MRS. GOODMAN,

I OFFER THIS STUDY OF

THE AUTHOR OF

MR. BADMAN

Printed in Great Britain for Hodder and Stoughton, Limited,
Richard Clay & Sons, Limited, Bungay, Suffolk.

General Preface

THE object of HODDER AND STOUGHTON'S
PEOPLE'S LIBRARY is to supply in brief form
simply written introductions to the study of
History, Literature, Biography and Science;
in some degree to satisfy that ever-increasing
demand for knowledge which is one of the
happiest characteristics of our time. The
names of the authors of the first volumes of
the Library are sufficient evidence of the fact
that each subject will be dealt with authorita-
tively, while the authority will not be of the
"dry-as-dust" order. Not only is it possible
to have learning without tears, but it is also
possible to make the acquiring of knowledge a thrilling and entertaining adventure.
HODDER AND STOUGHTON'S PEOPLE'S LIBRARY
will, it is hoped, supply this adventure.

Note

THIS book is an endeavour to summarise all that we know of Bunyan the man and to estimate him as a writer. A good deal has been discovered since Dr. Brown wrote his most valuable biography, to which I have constantly referred, in the edition published in 1918. Now, three hundred years since Bunyan was born, it may be well to devote to him a new study. I have to thank many for kind help: such as Sir Charles Firth, Professor Brett and Professor Bruce, of Cardiff, the Rev. Dr. Whitley and the Rev. Dr. Carnegie Simpson: the Editors of *The Times* and *The Guardian* for some passages from their columns: Miss Dorothea Beach for much help in copying and with the index: my publishers for their patience.

W. H. H.

Winchester,
  December, 1927.

Contents

PART I.—LIFE

PART II.—LITERATURE

THOSE who have not made themselves at home in the seventeenth century, probably when they think of it at all find their thoughts of England revolving round Charles I or Vandyke or Milton or Cromwell, according as their sympathies dictate. But when one looks below the surface, reads the books minutely, listens to the music diligently, one is tempted to rank beside these, for enduring influence, the names of Laud and Hobbes, of Purcell and Clarendon. And Disraeli would tell us of much obscurer men who, as he thinks, made the history behind the scenes. What we are still more apt to ignore are the humble, rough and rustic influences which made England the dull yet conquering country she was to become in the century which followed. The beautiful personages on the canvas of Vandyke, the exquisite grace of melody in the prose of Traherne or the notes of a Blest Pair of Sirens, the stately and romantic imagery of the English Church as John Inglesant saw it, the richness of Jeremy Taylor and the chiselled simplicity of George Herbert, fill the foreground of the picture. The fascination of the Stewarts is immortal. But behind these stars, still glittering in their courses through the memories of men, there was the rough, unpolished solidity of the English temper which emerges as you read the reminiscences of Aubrey, the photographic plays of the Caroline drama-tists, or the mixture of imagination with hard facts which marks the genius of John Bunyan. If you want to know what the common Englishman thought or what life the rustic lived, remote from licentious courts or the passion of poetry, you will find in " The Pilgrim's Progress " the record of an inspired yet ignorant and prejudiced tinker.

It is the vivid reality of Bunyan which brings him almost into the company of Shakespeare. Those two are the only English writers of the age about whom there is no touch of insincerity or precociousness. If Charles I loved Shakespeare, one feels that Shakespeare would have understood Bunyan, and if not loved at least pardoned him for his narrowness, as all understanding pardons. At least one eminent historian has regarded Cromwell as the typical Englishman. The contention is hard to justify. We might make the claim for Shakespeare because he saw and knew so much. One is tempted, if timidly, to make the claim for Bunyan because, like so many Englishmen, he saw not far but so clearly and so straight. Some words in which W. E. Henley described the poetry of Wilfrid Scawen Blunt, a writer poles apart indeed from Bunyan, come to mind as we think of him. Henley says of his subject that he was a man " who being set in a certain *milieu* has assimilated all of it he could and has produced the results before the world in terms distinguished enough to make them a lasting contribution to English letters." This is true of Bunyan, and truer still are some later words, which may well be applied to " The Pilgrim's Progress "—" whoso touches this book touches a man, and in him touches as much of his age as it was given him to see."

In November, 1628, John Bunyan was born at Elstow, about a mile from Bedford, where the town is now stretching out towards it, on the London road. His family can be traced back for centuries; and they were people who often got into trouble. Their wills show them to have had some little property; and the grandfather of John was able to leave to his executor " twelve pence in remembrance for his pains to be taken in seeing this my last Will and Testament duly and truly executed." Thomas, his son, the father of John, married at the age of twenty, in his parish church, Anne Pinney, who died

four years later; and on May 23, 1627, he
married again, the bride being Margaret
Bentley. Of the parents we know very little;
and of the family, that Bunyan spoke of
"the meanness and inconsiderableness of my
parents" and "for my family descent it was,
as is well known to many, of a low and
inconsiderable generation, my father's house
being of that rank that is meanest and most
despised of all the families in the land;
wherefore I have not here, as others, to
boast of noble blood or of any high-born
state, according to the flesh." Dr. Stebbing,
who edited Bunyan's works in 1862, tells us,
after the religious manner of his time, that
"there was nothing extraordinary in the
circumstance that a very famous and holy
man was the son of a tinker." Be that as
it may, it may be well to remove the preju-
dice which the familiar word seems to
arouse. Thomas Bunyan's will describes
him as a "braseyer," which is certainly a
more dignified word. But the word tinker

—Johnson says it means " a mender of old brass "—has nothing discreditable about it. Tinkers were not gipsies, as readers of Borrow and travellers in the Highlands of Scotland are tempted to think. Theirs is a very honourable trade, and it gives opportunity for study. I have myself seen a tinker driving his little cart and learning his Greek grammar at the same time, with a view to Holy Orders.

Bunyan's grandmother had " one brass pot " to bequeath : perhaps it had been mended by his father. She had also a " standing bed in the loft " : perhaps, like Shakespeare's bequest to his wife, the second-best bed.

So much for his ancestry : what of the country in which he was born ? Elstow, though now a pilgrimage centre, is still an unspoiled village, not much more than a mile from Bedford. It had an interesting history before Bunyan was born, for there was a Benedictine house there founded in

1078 by Judith, the niece of William the Conqueror and widow of the great English Earl Waltheof, who was beheaded on S. Giles's Hill, Winchester. Long a rich and honourable house, it fell on evil days. In the thirteenth century its church was used by the village. The connection became, it may be, too close, as an injunction of Bishop Longland in 1500 suggests. The western portion still survives as the parish church. A few points in the history of the nunnery are worth recalling. They throw some light on the sort of impressions Bunyan's childhood may have registered out of the village memories of the past and the talk of the "oldest inhabitants."

The Abbey of Elstow appears not to have had, in the early fifteenth century at least, more than twenty nuns. Visitations show that it was a poor house and could not keep up this number. The site was not attractive. The neighbouring town, it seems, did not take much interest in the nuns.

B

In 1442-3 the Elstow house was found to be in good order when the abbess and the convent of the monastery appeared before the Bishop. Some of the monks, it is true, complained of the eating of cooked meat and of capons when it was forbidden. The nuns even ate *adipata*—that is, food " with the blood." Though four-footed beasts could not be eaten, yet hens, being two-footed, one supposes could be. There were only thirteen nuns then, but they had a good allowance of beer. These thirteen poor old ladies, from different parts of England, and rather closely mewed up, are not likely to have had much influence locally.

On Saturday, January 17, 1421-2, Bishop Fleming was at Elstow; but though he finished his visitation in one day, his injunctions were very strict indeed. They followed those of Archbishop Courtenay in 1382, and were very stern against lodgers and the admission into any nun's room of any seculars or other men of religion. Nor

could any nun visit Bedford or the village
of Elstow, or wear silver pins in her hair or
silken gowns or several rings, but only one,
the ring of her profession.

The visitation of Bishop Longland in
1530 ordered

" that noo ladye remayne longer than
halff hoore after seven of the clock att
night and that noo man, preeste, ne
other, come into the said place called the
misericorde without speciall lycence of the
lady abbesse "; that " Katheryne Wingate
the said lady abbesse her chapleyn do not
suppe ne breke her faste in the buttry with
the stuard nor eny other secular person ";
" that noon of the religious susters doo
use or were here after ony such voyded
shoys, and that ther gownes and kyrtells
be clossed afore and not soo depe voyde
att the breste and noo more to use rede
stomachers but other sadder colers in the
same."

At the dissolution the inmates numbered

twenty-four. The good ladies receiving pensions were the abbess, £50 a year, and each nun, £2.

It seems to have been intended to use the church as a cathedral for the see of Bedford which Henry designed to found ; but nothing came of the project.

In June 1603 the Archbishop of Canterbury wrote to the Bishop of Lincoln " upon some special occasions me thereunto moving," desiring information, secretly from every parson, vicar and curate, as to the number of communicants in each parish, recusants, non-communicants, and pluralists, with other details, enough to make a sort of ecclesiastical Domesday.

A *Liber Cleri* exists in the Lincoln Diocesan Registry which contains the answers to this question. Of " Elstow *alias* Welstow," it says : " *Q.* P'ge approp. with a curat. *V.* Curat 8 li. stip. P. The King's Matie. *I* Robert Hundley, curat. *D.* Mr of Arts. P. a preacher, non Lic. *Beha.* good. *R.* est.

R. *Com.* 260. *Non-com*, 2 men, 4 women. *Recus* 1 man."

The church itself has been drastically restored. In the nineteenth century very many things which would have recalled the past were removed or destroyed. The plaster was taken off the walls, which in consequence assumed that naked and distracted appearance to create which seems to have been the main aim of many reforming architects of that period. The old pulpit remains, now put into a recess near a doorway which has been blocked up. From this Christopher Hall preached the sermon on Sabbath-breaking which disconcerted Bunyan. At the time of the restoration many graves were rifled, and some of their contents were preserved as curiosities. Several brasses remain, and some of them are interesting. A certain Dame Margery, who had had two husbands, died in 1427. Her brass shows her dog lying at her feet : its name, however, is not given, as is that of

Tiri at Deerhurst. There is also the brass
of Dame Margery's grand-daughter, Elizabeth Hervey, the last abbess but three, who
died in 1524. This has been much muti-
lated. The font is late perpendicular.
There are some rather pleasant vices at its
base. In this font, of course, John Bunyan
was baptised (November 30, 1628). His
own baptism is not recorded here, for the
parish register begins in 1641; but the
baptisms of his daughters, Mary and Elizabeth, 1650 and 1654, are entered.

At the west end of the church and below
its level is a vaulted chamber whose groined
roof is supported by a single pillar of Pur-
beck marble. This room was, no doubt,
part of the monastic buildings, probably
the Chapter House. The interesting point
about the tower is that it is separate from
the church. It stands to the north-west,
and, no doubt, through it access was had
to the cloisters of the abbey. The upper
part of it was added in the sixteenth century

as a bell chamber. None of the bells is earlier than the seventeenth century. The fifth bell, which has for inscription the alphabet (partly upside down), is called traditionally " Bunyan's Bell." He tells how fond he was of the vain practice of bell-ringing, so that even after he had given it up he used to go to look on till he became so frightened that he fled from the bell tower, fearing that the whole might fall on his head.

The Moot Hall stands upon the village green, where a fair was held from ancient times down to the nineteenth century. There, they say, Bunyan evolved his idea of " Vanity Fair." There he played tipcat, until he heard the voice which said, " Wilt thou leave thy sins and go to Heaven, or have thy sins and go to Hell? " Conversion was not immediate, for he considered that " I can but be damned, and if it must be so, I'd as soon be damned for many sins as to be damned for few."

Little of the abbey buildings remains.

There is what is called the abbey doorway, but this (and much else) must surely have been built many years after the dissolution, when the building was the private dwelling-house of the Radclyffs, to whom the King gave it at the dissolution. From them it passed to the Hillendons and from them at the very end of the eighteenth century to the Whitbreads, by whom about a century later it was given to the parish for a vicarage. Some have rashly supposed that this house gave Bunyan his idea of the "House Beautiful," but no doubt this was really Houghton House at Ampthill.

What is now called "The Moot Hall" (but I do not know how old the name is, and whether really medieval) is a delightful brick-and-timber building in the wide field across the road which leads to the church. The lower part is now a carpenter's shop; the upper is fitted with benches for a Bunyanite congregation or school; and it is visited by pilgrims from all over the world. So is the cottage he lived in in his later years, decently plastered outside, four windows only on the front, two above and two below, with a door between—all very homely and comfortable. But they say that this is only a modern fake, and that the real cottage was pulled down about 1830, and the very forge that Bunyan worked at destroyed. The house in which he was born, at Harrowden, has long perished.

In Bedford Bunyan's meeting-house, founded in 1650, has long passed away, as has the county prison by the bridge, in which he was incarcerated. He ministered in that chapel from 1672 to 1688. It has been replaced by a somewhat pretentious and certainly not beautiful building of the style in which the nineteenth century was prone to indulge. This has many commodious rooms for the minister and his classes; and there is, on the first floor at the back, an interesting museum, where are many early editions of Bunyan's books. I noticed

"Dirt Wiped Off," 1672, among them. There is also a pretty little cabinet of his, his chair, his walking-stick—given by his great-granddaughter, a jug of dark German ware, and a pot which he may have shaved or drunk from. And transplanted thither are the old belfry doors from Elstow, through which he must often have passed when he was a bell-ringer. Close to this Bunyan *enclave*, which occupies a considerable space, is the Norman church of S. Cuthbert, which he must have known well. The ground plan is particularly interesting and somewhat uncommon, but its interior is now completely spoiled by restoration. The other churches in Bedford have great interest, notably the splendid S. Paul's, of the fifteenth century, and S. Peter's, partly of the eleventh, and the fine S. John Baptist, with a good (I suppose modern) image on the tower, and presumably alms-houses adjoining.

Now as to details of S. Peter's Church

sceptics may be a little doubtful; so I will merely quote what the present-day local personages say. It is this :

" It does not require any great amount of archæological knowledge in order to see that S. Peter's Church is of very ancient date—its looks proclaim it : traces of fire may still be seen resulting from the Danish attack on the town in 1010; fragments of old-time workmanship remain in the shape of a fine Saxon doorway in the belfry of the tower; and a beautiful Norman porch (with an outer covering to shield it from the weather) on the south side of the building."

Of a still-remaining relic of antiquity in the centre of the town Mr. Farrer's history, published in 1926, speaks more precisely : doubtless more precisely than can be proved.

" The old stone pulpit [standing in the corner of the Trinity Chapel of S. Paul's] has great traditions. It has voiced every school of theology and Church polity for at least 400 years, and probably dates back to the XIVth century. Andrew Denays, Theodore Crowley, John Bradshaw, John Burton, John Bunyan, all have occupied it."

Thus briefly we may recall what Bunyan must have seen, and the relics of him which survive. But, certainly, if we say " Si monumentum quaeris," it must be to the books he wrote that we direct attention. There are no surviving tokens which show, even as dimly as those of Shakespeare show, what manner of man he was. What do we learn from himself about his upbringing and his early years ?

On the whole, Bunyan, and his biographers after him, may be considered to have disparaged his parentage : it is one form of the pride that comes to those who rise to eminence in the world's eye. He admits, however, that he was put to school " to learn me both to read and write; the which I also attained, according to the rate of other poor men's children." He says he soon forgot all he had learned, but this must certainly be an exaggeration, or he could not have become the " man of letters " that he was. We ask, and cannot get a certain answer, where was Bunyan at school; was there a village school at Elstow? There may have been a relic of the monastic one. Or was he at that famous grammar school of Bedford? We do not know. There was a free school, not far off, at Houghton Conquest, and there was the great (not yet famous) school of Belford, but both seem to have fallen on evil days. Indeed, at the very time when Bunyan should have been at school, the master of the latter is found to have been of a most discreditable character, neglecting his duties, or making up for the lack of teaching by cruelty, and misspending his time in ale-houses.

What education, wherever he got it, did Bunyan receive, then? Since the time of Elyot's " Governour " (1531) and the in-

fluence of Erasmus, who came to count
himself almost as an Englishman, theory
had been made to supplement practice and
the rule of thumb, by which no doubt English
children had been taught the little they
learnt in country villages. These eminent
personages were, of course, concerned chiefly
with the higher classes. Elyot would begin
with the kind of behaviour expected from
gentlefolk : " Incontinent as soon as they
can speak it behoveth with most pleasant
allurings to instil into them sweet manner
and virtuous customs " ; and education in
book learning should begin at a very early
age.

By 1607 a further advance was made by
Cleland's " The Instruction of a Young
Nobleman." But it would be long before
these exalted notions could sink down to
the poorer classes. If we were sure that
Bunyan went to Bedford Grammar School
we should be likely to conclude that he was
able, like Shakespeare, to acquire little

Latin and less Greek. But what could be learnt in a village school? That would depend upon the teacher; and Bunyan's teacher, whoever he was, certainly taught the child how to read English with understanding and to write it with directness. The grammar schools, however, cannot have been without their influence on the village schools, for the village teachers must have been taught in the town schools. If old Beeston is to be believed, Shakespeare himself taught in a village school. And what could not a clever boy learn from him? Of course country boys, where possible, went into the towns, and certainly Bunyan may, for however short a time, have been one of such scholars. It must be remembered that till very much later than the early seventeenth century the children of gentle and simple folk were taught together. Many squires and parsons at least till the nineteenth century (and why not now?) would send their boys to local grammar

schools. No doubt the main thing then sought
was a grounding in religion.   Then, as now,
parents generally showed reluctant restless-
ness when they approached the thought of
religious instruction, and left it to teachers
who were supposed, perhaps with more
justice than to-day, to be able to teach
from the heart as well as from the head,
and at least with belief if not always with
intelligence.   If Bunyan learnt any classical
literature at all, it is not likely that he was
instructed in the spirit which came to the
front with Puritanism. Said Dell, Master
of Caius, as to the teaching of children—
" they should learn the Greek and Latin
tongues especially from Christians and so
without the lies, fables, follies, vanities,
whoredoms, lust, pride, revenge, etc., of
the heathen, especially seeing neither their
words nor their phrases are meet for
Christians to take in their mouth; and
most necessary it is, that Christians should
forget the names of their gods and muses,

which were but devils and damned creatures,
and all their mythology and fabulous inventions, and let them all go to Satan from
whence they came." Would Bunyan have
said quite this? Would he forget all these
abominations? Or had he never learnt?

When Bunyan was fifteen his mother
died, and soon afterwards his sister Margaret; soon again his father married a new
wife. Dr. Brown thought this an indignity
to the mother's memory, and that the lad
must have resented it and become estranged
from his father and his home. This, of
course, is only a guess. Let us offer another.
The "Bonion of Elsto," who found three
rooks in a nest, "all white as milk and not
a black feather on them," and thought this
important enough to tell the rector of
Houghton Conquest, may well have been
of a poetic nature, and have put romantic
thoughts into his son's mind and made him
feel that it was a call of honour to enter the
Civil War as a combatant. This he most

c

likely did within a very few months of his mother's death. No doubt he enlisted voluntarily : the time had not yet come when the Parliament had to rely on pressed men.

Bunyan's army service has long been a puzzle to historians. We know that he served in the Civil War. The proof is to be found in his own writings :

" When I was a soldier," says he, " I with others were drawn out to go to such a place to besiege it ; but when I was just ready to go, one of the company desired to go in my room, which when I had consented he took my place ; and coming to the siege, as he stood sentinel, he was shot into the head with a musket bullet, and died."

This may have been at the siege of Grafton House, in South Northants, not very far from Bedford, or later, at Aylesbury or Farnham. But one of the early Lives, on which very little reliance can be

placed, says that the siege was that of
Leicester, and it is known that some of
the Newport Pagnell men were there,
defending the town against the troops of
Prince Rupert.

But that does not carry us far; so short
a way, indeed, that till lately no one has
been sure on which side he fought, and
J. A. Froude was almost inclined to think
that he was in the Royalist army. But
the mystery did not remain unsolved.
The evidence is to be found in three muster
rolls discovered in the Record Office by Mr.
E. G. Atkinson in 1896.* One of these is
a list of Colonel Cockayne's company dated
November 30, 1644. This was part of the
garrison of Newport Pagnell, of which
Sir Samuel Luke was governor. He, by the
way, was a stern disciplinarian. He arrested
two of Fairfax's captains in 1645 because
they had their own conventicle and refused

* Facsimiles were published in *The Presbyterian*,
March 3, 1898.

to join in a thanksgiving for Naseby. They would not have won the admiration of Bunyan, certainly, for when the thanksgiving was held, they went off " with a company of ignorant women, and a young boy, and seven men more, whereby the witness of a company of pots and jugs they exercised their gifts." Not a very strict conventicle doubtless ; but Fairfax insisted on their being released.* Yet it may well be that it was in the army that Bunyan acquired the desire to preach. One Chillenden, a lieutenant, published " Preaching without Ordination " in 1647, and Edwards in "Gangraena" states that a young soldier said to him that the soldiers " if they have not leave to preach they will not fight." Bunyan was certainly very far from being an anti-militarist. His name also appears on a roll (March 22, 1645) of Major Boulton's company, and there it is found till May 27, 1645 : this was another company in the

* See Firth, " Cromwell's Army," p. 336.

Newport Pagnell garrison. On June 17, 1647, when Lieutenant-Colonel O'Hara's company was mustered at Newport Pagnell, his name again appears.* Probably his continuous military service ceased in August 1646, when the Newport Pagnell garrison was disbanded. His appearance (says Sir Charles Firth) in the list of O'Hara's company probably indicates a fresh engagement.

Charles O'Hara was a captain in Colonel Robert Hammond's regiment in the New Model from 1645 to 1647. Captain O'Hara was one of the officers who in 1647 was willing to engage for service in Ireland, and several other officers and about 400 privates in Hammond's regiment followed his example. He was ordered to march his men to Newport Pagnell as a convenient rendezvous, and they were to be organised into a new regiment under Colonel Owen O'Conolly, of which O'Hara was to be lieutenant-colonel.

* I owe all these facts to Sir Charles Firth.

The company never went to Ireland, because this provisional regiment was disbanded by order of Parliament made July 21, 1647. It would seem then, in default of any further discovery, that two years of garrison service at most was the sum of Bunyan's experience, in addition to about a couple of months in an abortive regiment intended for Ireland. But he always had a soldier's spirit.

So far we do not know of much religious feeling in the young Bunyan. When he wrote his autobiography in " Grace Abounding to the Chief of Sinners " (by whom he meant himself) twenty years later, in 1666, he took an extremely gloomy view of his early life. One of his biographers from this believes that he was " plunged in a sea of iniquity," and fancies that because, while he had (perhaps) given up church-going, he still came to the tower and rang the bells, he must have taken a " moody pleasure " in tolling for the " departure of

some struggling soul." He had now returned to Elstow, and married—we do not
know whom; but we know that she was a
pious woman who was always telling her
husband how pious her father was; and that
is not unlikely to have irritated him and
caused him to continue his lurid language
and profane ways. Also he tells us that they
had not so much as a dish or a spoon between
them. (Did they eat from the pie and with
their fingers? Imaginative minds, like
Bunyan's, are prone to exaggeration.)

There can be little doubt that Bunyan
exaggerated his own ungodliness at this
time or that his wife exercised a good
influence over him. She brought him two
pious books, a dull one called "The Plain
Man's Pathway to Heaven," and a very
beautiful one called "The Practice of
Piety," dedicated to Charles I when Prince
of Wales. But it was some time before
Bunyan began to practise piety, beyond
going to church twice a Sunday, which was

at the least a very good beginning. What he says about himself, twenty years later, is this :

" I fell in with the religion of the times to go to church twice a day, very devoutly to say and sing as the others did, yet retaining my wicked life. Withal I was so overrun with the spirit of superstition that I adored with great devotion even all things, both the high place, priest, clerk, vestment, service and what else belonging to the Church, counting all things holy therein contained, and especially the priest and clerk most happy and without doubt greatly blessed. This conceit grew so strong in my spirit, that had I but seen a priest, though never so sordid and debauched in his life, I should find my spirit fall under him, reverence, and be knit to him. Their name, their garb, and work did so intoxicate and bewitch me."

The vicar of Elstow was Christopher Hall. It is probably of his services before the Civil War that Bunyan speaks ; yet in spite of the silencing of the Prayer Book it may be that Hall, who held the benefice till 1664, kept up as much as possible of the old manner in the dark days. But the whole tendency of Bedfordshire religious feeling was against the strict obedience to the Prayer Book which Laud endeavoured to enforce.

Bedfordshire was one of the counties which accepted the English Reformation eagerly, and many of the people especially did so for its Protestant affirmations. The Church's censures were often disregarded after the "change of religion." The visitations show repeated attempts to enforce the civil penalties of excommunication. Dr. John Brown found in the Act books of the Bedford Archdeaconry many instances of this, but set them forth with some exaggeration and considerable confusion of dates. The worst instances of neglect and disobedience certainly occurred before the Reformation. But it is clear

from such instances as bear-baiting in
Woburn church and cock-fightings at Knot-
tingley, with at least the connivance of the
parish priests, that the restoration of discipline by Laud was greatly needed. In
1612 at S. Paul's, Bedford, Parson Adams
(a prototype, maybe, of Fielding's famous
man) cried out, " We are well freed from
the Bonners and butchers of Christ's lambs ;
but we have still fleecers enough—too
many—that love to see learning follow
Homer with a staff and a wallet. Every
gentleman thinks the priest mean, but the
priest's means hath made many a gentleman." So late as 1635 a visitation sermon
at Ampthill shows that the country squires
were a great hindrance to religion : " The
great men do send God's messengers upon
their base errands, place them below their
serving men, esteem them below their
parasites." The Elizabethan reformation
had not raised the social condition of the
clergy.

At Laud's visitation in 1634 Bedfordshire was found " the most tainted part "
of the vast Lincoln diocese. The metro-
political visitation revealed dreadful dis-
order, and in many villages total neglect
of the decent order of the Church. The
officials employed, deputies of deputies,
were often hasty, irritable, and unduly
interfering; but strong measures were
really needed. It was not to be wondered
if one commissary lost his temper with a
senile parson, a hundred years old, and
called him " an old owl." Reforms too
often cause resentment, notably when they
have been too long delayed. In the Long
Parliament none were more vociferous than
the Bedfordshire men : they were prominent among those who declared the making
churches clean and services reverent to be
" scandalous and superstitious innovations."

The famous Bedfordshire petition presented by Sir John Burgoyne, representa-
tive of a famous family which has long lived

at Sutton, was supported, when it was brought to the House of Commons, by the high sheriff, esquires, gentlemen, ministers, freeholders and others, inhabitants of the county," some two thousand persons, it was said; " four in rank with their protestations in their hats." A fine show they must have made as they passed through Elstow : and Bunyan, the tinker's boy, was twelve years old, perhaps the most impressionable age in a lifetime. This was a fine example of Pym's method of over-awing Parliament. The times of the Act against tumultuous petitions are still far off.

Bunyan, we may safely say, was not prejudiced in favour of the orthodox teaching of the Church of England. It happened to him, as to so many others, that, not fully understanding it, when presented, maybe, in a stiff and dry form, he ran to the English version of the Bible, and, taking both Testaments together, extracted a panacea of his own mixing for the healing of his spiritual infirmities. He thought, no doubt, that he should resort to the Lord and not to the physician. He was not acquainted with the age-long records of experience " by which saints, under the inspiration of the Spirit of Christ, had formed the theology of the Christian Church." He needed, and he attained, a real conversion of the soul. We may be sure that he speaks truly when he says that he had never been guilty of sexual immorality. But the tongue can be a world of iniquity; and he says, " Even as a child I had few equals in cursing, swearing, lying and blaspheming the holy name of God." He shocked even profane persons. Modern biographers regard this profanity as a manifestation of spiritual struggle. A sermon on Sunday observance struck him to the soul. He veered back and forward as to playing games on " the Sabbath," as Puritans often called it. One day when

he was playing " cat " (tip-cat, I presume)
he had a dreadful warning :

" A voice did suddenly dart from heaven
into my soul, which said, ' Wilt thou leave
thy sins and go to heaven, or have thy sins
and go to hell ? '   At this I was put to an
exceeding maze.   Wherefore, leaving my
cat upon the ground, I looked up to heaven,
and was as if I had with the eyes of my
understanding seen the Lord Jesus looking
down upon me, as being very hotly dis-
pleased with me."

He gave up tip-cat, it seems, but he kept
up bell-ringing for a while.   Then he began
to consider that also to be wicked, perhaps
because of the custom among bell-ringers,
which has by no means died out even now,
of leaving the tower the moment their
laborious exercise is over, and trooping off
before divine service begins.   Yet he certainly never ceased to love the sound of
bells, for when his pilgrims drew nigh to
the Celestial City they heard the bells, and

when they were inside, " all the bells in the
city rang for joy." After bell-ringing he
gave up the old pleasant folk-dancing, but
not immediately. When he did so at last
he said to himself, " God cannot choose but
be pleased with me."

How little did this mortification bring
him towards God. Still he fretted and
wondered. The sermon against Sabbath-
breaking stirred him to the marrow till he
had had a good dinner and forgot it. But
while he was filling his belly with sin, as he
fancied, he was always full of more fears
than wars or women have. " And I am
very confident," he says in later life, " that
this temptation of the devil is more usual
among poor creatures than many are aware
of, even to overrun the spirits with a
scurvy and seared frame of heart and
benumbing of conscience ; which frame he
stilly and slily supplieth with such despair,
that though not much guilt attendeth souls,
yet they continually have a secret con-

clusion within them that there is hope for them ; for they loved sins, therefore after them they will go."

" Bunyan " (says Walter Scott) " had ere now formed to himself an hypothesis accounting for the blasphemous thoughts which distracted his mind, imputing them, in short, to the immediate suggestion of the devil ; and how he clung to it we may discover from one striking passage in Christian's progress through the valley of the shadow of death.

" One thing I would not let slip ; I took notice that now poor Christian was so confounded, that he did not know his own voice ; and thus I perceived it : just when he was come over against the mouth of the burning pit, one of the Wicked ones got behind him, and stepped up softly to him, and whisperingly suggested many grievous blasphemies to him, which he verily thought had proceeded from his own mind. This put Christian more to it than any thing he met with before, even to think he should now blaspheme him that he loved so much before : yet, if he could have helped it, he would not have done it; but he had not the discretion either to stop his ears, or to know from whence these blasphemies came."

Thus furnished with a theory to account for the black suggestions which (as he says) he dared not to utter, either with word or pen, Bunyan was now taught by his mistaken pastor to look for a counterbalance in the equally direct inspirations of heaven. So strong is the power of the human imagination that he who seriously expects to see miracles does not long expect them in vain. He spent hours in debating whether, in the strength of newly-adopted faith, he should not command the puddles on the highway to be dry, and the dry places to be wet; and if he shrunk from so presumptuous an experiment, it was only because he had not the courage to think of facing the despair which must have ensued, if the sign, which he would fain have demanded, had been refused to his prayer."

D

" Mr. Southey " (continues Scott) " thus describes his condition, while engaged in balancing the support and comfort which he received from heaven with the discountenance and criminal suggestions inspired by the enemy of mankind :

" ' Shaken continually thus by the hot and cold fits of a spiritual ague, his imagination was wrought to a state of excitement in which its own shapings became vivid as realities, and affected him more forcibly than impressions from the external world. He heard sounds as in a dream ; and as in a dream held conversations which were inwardly audible, though no sounds were uttered, and had all the connexion and coherency of an actual dialogue. Real they were to him in the impression which they made, and in their lasting effect ; and even afterwards, when his soul was at peace, he believed them, in cool and sober reflection, to have been more than natural. Some days he was much " followed," he says, by these words of the Gospel, " Simon, Simon, behold Satan hath desired to have you ! " He knew that it was a voice from within,—

and yet it was so articulately distinct, so
loud, and called, as he says, so strongly
after him, that once in particular, when the
words Simon! Simon! rung in his ears,
he verily thought some man had called to
him from a distance behind, and though it
was not his name, supposed nevertheless
that it was addressed to him, and looked
round suddenly to see by whom. As this
had been the loudest, so it was the last time
that the call sounded in his ears; and he
imputes it to his ignorance and foolishness
at that time, that he knew not the reason
of it; for soon, he says, he was feelingly
convinced that it was sent from heaven, as
an alarm, for him to provide against the
coming storm,—a storm which " handled
him twenty times worse than all he had
met with before." ' "

Yet he sought to live a good life: his
outward living was all holy—men would
say, " a right honest man," yet never satisfied with himself: a " poor painted hypocrite," he says, for all the while, so he
thought, he was ignorant of Jesus Christ

and going about to establish his own righteousness.

Then comes a beautiful little picture of a happy, maybe a real, conversion, because it spoke of simplicity and beauty joined to goodness, which indeed make on earth the paradise of God. Thus Bunyan tells of it:

" Upon a day, the good providence of God called me to Bedford, to work on my calling; and in one of the streets of that town I came where there were three or four poor women sitting at a door in the sun, talking about the things of God; and being now willing to hear them discourse, I drew near to hear what they said, for I was now a brisk talker also myself in the matter of religion; but I may say, ' I heard, but I understood not; ' for they were far above, out of my reach. Their talk was about a new birth, the work of God on their hearts; also how they were convinced of their miserable state by nature. They talked how God had visited their souls with his love in the Lord Jesus, and with what words and promises they had been

refreshed, comforted, and supported against
the temptations of the devil : moreover,
they reasoned of the suggestions and temptations of Satan in particular; and told to
each other by which they had been afflicted,
and how they were borne up under his
assaults. They also discoursed of their
own wretchedness of heart, of their unbelief; and did contemn, slight, and abhor
their own righteousness as filthy and in-
sufficient to do them any good.

" And methought they spake as if you
did make them speak; they spake with
such pleasantness of scripture language,
and with such appearance of grace in all
they said, that they were to me as if they
had found a new world, as if they were
' people that dwelt alone, and were not
to be reckoned among their neighbours '
(Numb. xxiii. 9)." *

So there came of this talk at last a very
great softness and tenderness of heart.
So soon as the beauty of holiness entered

* The " Complete Works of John Bunyan," [ed.
1862] Vol. I. pp. 8 and 9.

into his mind, which had before been filled only with its sternness, he cast off his evil companions. His chief friend among them, a truly wicked man who from the midst of disgusting sinfulness answered his reproof with such a quip as a friend might have rejoiced in—" What would the devil do for company were it not for such as I am? "

He had learnt from " a poor man that made profession of religion " to read the Bible. It was a step forward. But then his religious intimate deserted him. " He turned," says Bunyan, " a most devilish Ranter, and gave himself up to all manner of filthiness, especially uncleanness." Though he at once left his company, the man's poisonous opinion must have added to the distress of one who was struggling betwixt good and evil, often in despair, yet sometimes bright with the light of God shining on him. It was now that he began " to look into the Bible with new eyes, and read as I never did before." Yet at first it seems to have proved more puzzle than comfort. What sort of faith was his? What did he mean by being saved, as Bishop Westcott is said to have asked the brusque inquirer? Did ever any trust in God and were confounded? But that text, when he found that it was only in Ecclesiasticus, seemed unsafe, and only daunted him at first. From Genesis to "the Revelations" (as he, like most ignorant folk, calls the book) he read and searched and was not satisfied. More loathsome he became in his own eyes than a toad. Many months passed, and when he tearfully wondered whether he was among the elect, he could find nothing shown him whether he was called already or should be hereafter. It was a piteous state. There are few more distressful pages in all religious history than those in which Bunyan tells of his slow and struggling ascent towards God. Yet it cannot be doubted that he was rising steadily : falling now and then, but never

deprived in his most despondent moments
of the guidance of the Holy Ghost.

If the first decided step in advance was
that talk with the Bedford women, the
second came when he made the acquaintance
of John Gifford, who was their minister.
Gifford was a remarkable man, a " brand
plucked from the burning " as that age,
and later ones, would say.   The Dictionary of National Biography ignores
him, but he must have been a most capable
and notable man.   A " converted Royalist
major " Dr. Brown calls him, one who had
had " great extravagance of mind and wild-
ness of heart."   In 1655 he was admitted,
after what form of ordination we do not
know for certain, but as a minister of the
Baptists, to the rectory of S. John's,
Bedford, and the mastership of the Hospital.   Now the roll of Baptist members
of this church had been kept from 1650,
and on it the name of John Bunyan stands
nineteenth.   From two years before 1655 he

was among Gifford's flock. His friends told
Gifford of him, and he says that the converted major "also took occasion to talk
with me and was willing to be well-per-
suaded of me, though I think but from little
grounds." It seems that Gifford baptised
Bunyan—though he had, of course, been
christened as a baby—and Southey thinks
this took place in the Ouse, "for the
Baptists sought rather than shunned pub-
licity at that time." In Featley's curious
pamphlet, written ten years before—of
which more anon—there is a curious wood-
cut representing such baptisms, no doubt
slanderously, including that of a "hemero-
baptist," which apparently means one
who daily bathed out of doors: "quia
quotidie baptizantur," says Featley.

Gifford died on September 21, 1656,
leaving a valedictory letter to his flock
which Southey warmly praises: it dis-
couraged separation, but this probably
means separation from his Baptist flock.

Before Gifford's death, and after the birth of his two children, Mary and Elizabeth, Bunyan moved into Bedford, and became a formal member of the Baptist body.

IN the sixteenth century there was contention deep and widespread about religious
changes. In the seventeenth there was
turmoil almost as persistent about religious
settlement. When Mary reigned hundreds
were burnt to death for their often unfixed
and incoherent religious opinions; men
looked at the faith from different angles:
some were revolutionary, some historical,
some ebullient, some ascetic. Without were
fightings, within were fears. Morals as well
as theology seemed to be in the melting pot.
It appeared much easier to be religious than
to be good: character as well as opinion
seemed in perpetual flux. There seemed
no longer to be bounds for conduct any
more than for intellect or investigation.
In the seventeenth century England's posi-

tion was coming to be solid. Religious opinions were still manifold and eccentric. Warfare, indeed, had not ceased, but it was not for a Pilgrimage of Grace but for Ship Money and a Grand Remonstrance. Politics and religion were still close linked together. Yet it was for the first, not the second, that blood mounted to the horse-bridles. No longer were men careless, like the great Elizabethans, of the fundamentals of morality. The things men debated in the sixteenth century (as in the twentieth) without a blush were veiled in the seventeenth in decent reticence. There was a basal agreement as to what was good and what was bad. The great Elizabethans often seemed to wonder if anything were good or ill save as very unstable thinking made it so. The Cavaliers and Puritans had no doubt at all as to the sharp line that divided God from Devil, and if their feet wandered from the straight path they well knew that they had gone astray. The

Elizabethan said, " This is a boundless world, and my passions are boundless. I do not know if there is such a thing as damnation." His son and grandson said, " I know what is wrong, and will do it if I wish and be damned."

That is where Charles II differs from Queen Elizabeth.

There lies this difference between John Bunyan and his contemporaries and men perhaps greater than they. The Reformation had at last made men clear about morals, and their feet were planted on firm ground.

In the struggle against a blind and cruel fate, the struggle which often seems hopeless and yet never fails, lies the true life of man. Against this dark and brutal power there is ever struggling the vital spark, in humanity, yet above it, which sets the individual on his feet, though in the very midst of danger and despond, which refuses to be crushed, which cries aloud for survival and victory. And this some call individuality, and some the *élan vital;* and some know it as the Eternal Spirit of the living God.

There is a knowledge constantly springing up among men, sometimes, as in the days of the Great War, affecting companies, masses, even nations, with an overpowering force, that over the world there stands somewhere a stupendous force, unmoral, crushing, relentless, before which hearts fail, lives are shattered, characters crumble into dust. Some call it Fate, some circumstance, some Devil. Again and again men singly and even in masses seem helpless before it, and faith, goodness, mercy appear to be blotted from the map of life. To feel this is agony, yet not to perceive it marks a condition where man is soulless and irreclaimable.

Here to-day we may feel ourselves akin to John Bunyan. The soul-crisis is real. He passed through years of struggle : very slowly indeed did he climb the Delectable

Mountains. His was an age very different from the century before, and religious contest, confusion, retrogression, advance, were on different lines.

From his acquaintance, then, with John Gifford we may date the beginning of Bunyan's acceptance of opinions which diverged more and more widely from those in which he had been brought up. We do not know in what theology he had been nurtured. It seems more than probable that he received no systematic religious teaching at all. He picked up his theology in scraps. The first teacher he mentions as profoundly influencing him is Martin Luther. The German friar's doctrine of salvation by faith most naturally attracted him, for he felt that he could make nothing, amid his surging temptations, of his own works. When he looked round upon the best of his neighbours he was tempted to reassure himself by thinking, " I have faith if thou hast works." We do not know how much of Luther he read. Many books were translated, and little of the character of their author was known. In some respects there was close affinity between Bunyan and his German teacher. Each was thoroughly a man of the people. Each had the terrible trial of religious depression, and in agony heard voices and visualised devils. Each was a man of irrepressible energy, of genuine feeling, of passionate enthusiasm rising to religious ecstasy. But Bunyan, when he wrote, was never tainted by the revolting coarseness which makes Luther at times worthy to be called Martin Luther Coprostom. Foul words fled from Bunyan when he became the soldier of Jesus Christ. Gradually he drew near to one in particular among the many sectarian bodies which ran riot in the early years of the interregnum.

But still he was not at peace. Five or six years more, apparently, passed till he was fully happy in his faith : years, some of them passed in the companionship of

Gifford, some after his guide was removed from him. It may well be that his doubts and distresses did not leave him till he felt himself called, five or six years after he was "awakened," to minister to others. Sometimes he heard the voice of Christ calling him to the happiness of acceptance. Sometimes Satan seemed to be the conqueror in the continual conflicts which raged about his soul. Thus he writes once :

"Now was the battle won, and down fell I, as a bird that is shot from the top of a tree, into great guilt and fearful despair. Thus getting out of my bed, I went moping into the field; but, God knows, with as heavy a heart as mortal man, I think, could bear; where, for the space of two hours, I was like a man bereft of life, and as now past all recovery, and bound over to eternal punishment.

"And withal, that Scripture did seize upon my soul, ' —or profane person, as Esau, who, for one morsel of meat sold his birthright : for ye know, how that after-

E

wards, when he would have inherited the blessing, he was rejected; for he found no place of repentance, though he sort it carefully with tears ' (Heb. xii. 16, 17).

" Now was I as one bound; I felt myself shut up unto the judgment to come; nothing now for two years together would abide with me but damnation, and an expectation of damnation : I say, nothing now would abide with me but this, save some few moments for relief, as in the sequel you will see.

" These words were to my soul like fetters of brass to my legs, in the continual sound of which I went for several months together."

" Sometimes, indeed, I should have a touch from that in Luke xxii. 32 : ' I have prayed for thee, that thy faith fail not '; but it would not abide upon me; neither could I indeed, when I considered my state, find ground to conceive in the least that there should be the root of that grace within me, having sinned as I had done. Now was I torn and rent in a heavy case, for many days together." *

* " Complete Works of Bunyan," Vol. I. pp. 19–20.

But then there was the alternation of a gracious peace from God. Bunyan's story gives no countenance to the idea of an "instantaneous conversion": rather he was continually falling into despair and rising again in hope. Yet there is an occasion which may be called the climax.

Mr. J. A. Froude, who was an artist in epitomising (though not always accurately), thus compresses what Bunyan wrote : *

"As I was passing in the field," he goes on, " I heard the sentence, thy righteousness is in heaven; and methought I saw, with the eyes of my soul, Jesus Christ at God's right hand, there I say, as my righteousness, so that wherever I was, or whatever I was doing, God could not say of me He wants my righteousness, for that was just before Him. Now did my chains fall off my legs indeed. I was loosed from my affliction and irons, my temptations also fled away, so that from that time those dreadful

* " Bunyan," J. A. Froude, pp. 50, 51, abridged from Bunyan's Works, Vol. I. pp. 30–31.

Scriptures of God left off to trouble me. Now went I home rejoicing for the grace and love of God. Christ of God is made unto us wisdom and righteousness, and sanctification, and redemption. I now lived very sweetly at peace with God through Christ. Oh! methought, Christ, Christ! There was nothing but Christ before my eyes. I was not now only looking upon this and the other benefits of Christ apart, as of His blood, burial and resurrection, but considered Him as a whole Christ. All those graces that were now green in me were yet but like those cracked groats and fourpence halfpennies which rich men carry in their purses, while their gold is in their trunks at home. Oh! I saw my gold was in my trunk at home in Christ my Lord and Saviour. The Lord led me into the mystery of union with the Son of God, that I was joined to Him, that I was flesh of His flesh. If He and I were one, His righteousness was mine, His merits mine, His victory mine. Now I could see myself in heaven and earth at once; in heaven by my Christ, though on earth by my body and person."

Scott thought that in a species of vision or waking reverie it was that Bunyan contrasted his own condition with that of the Baptists and so resolved to join them.

" I saw," says Bunyan, " as if they were on the sunny side of some high mountain, there refreshing themselves with the pleasant beams of the sun, while I was shivering and shrinking in the cold, afflicted with frost, snow and dark clouds. Methought also betwixt me and them, I saw a wall that did compass about this mountain; now through this wall my soul did greatly desire to pass; concluding that if I could, I would even go into the very midst of them, and there also comfort myself with the heat of their sun. About this wall I thought myself to go again and again, still prying as I went, to see if I could find some way or passage, by which I might enter therein; but none could I find for some time. At the last I saw, as it were, a narrow gap, like a little doorway in the wall, through which I attempted to pass. Now the passage being very strait and narrow, I made many offers to get in, but all in vain, even until I was well-nigh quite beat out by striving to get in. At last with great striving, methought I at first did get in my head; and after that, by a sideling striving, my shoulders, and my whole body: then was I exceeding glad, went and sat down in the midst of them, and so was comforted with the light and heat of their sun. Now the mountain and wall, etc. were thus made out to me. The mountain signified the Church of the living God: the sun that shone thereon, the comfortable shining of his merciful face on them that were within: the wall, I thought, was the word, that did make separation between the Christians and the world; and the gap which was in the wall, I thought, was Jesus Christ, who is the way to God the Father. But forasmuch as the passage was wonderful narrow, even so narrow that I could not but with great difficulty enter in thereat, it shewed me that none could enter into life, but those that were in downright earnest; and unless also they left the wicked world behind them; for here was only room for body and soul, but not for body and soul and sin." *

We seem, in our record, to be like Bunyan himself, continually turning back, yet we advance, however slowly. By 1655, at least, he had become firm in his membership of the Baptists in their Bedford congregation, and was thought of to become one of their ministers. What did this involve?

The opinion of ordinary English people as to the preaching of unlearned folk is very well illustrated by a not too well-known tract of Thomas Hall, writ from his study in King's Norton and addressed "to the Lay-Preachers at Henley, War-wick, Aulcester &c., and to all their Factors, Favourers, Followers and Abettors." The author by no means belonged to the "High Church" party: he had refused to read

* Southey's "Life of John Bunyan," pp. 471-2. Here we find at least suggestions of "The Pilgrim's Progress."

the Book of Sports and had been threatened by the Episcopal party " for Nonconformity," plundered by the Cavaliers and five times their prisoner : now he was " set upon by the Sectaries," but was none the less determined to show the errors of the Anabaptists in England. The title explains the argument: it well deserves quoting in full.

" The Pulpit Guarded with xvii Arguments proving The Unlawfulness, Sinfulness and Danger of suffering Private persons to take upon them Publike Preaching, and expounding the Scriptures without a Call; as being contrary to the Word of God, contrary to the practice of all Reformed Churches, contrary to the Three and twentieth Article of Religion, contrary to two Ordinances of Parliament, and contrary to the judgement of a whole Jury of learned, judicious, pious Divines, both Forraign and Domestick. Occasioned by a Dispute at Henly in Arden in Warwick-shire, Aug. 20. 1650.

Against {
Lawrence Williams, a Nailor-Pub-
like-Preacher.
Tho. Palmer, a Baker-Preacher.
Tho. Hunde, a Plough-Wright-
Publike-Preacher.
Henry Oakes, a Weaver-Preacher.
Hum. Rogers (lately) a Bakers-
Boy-Publike-Preacher.
}

Here you have all their Arguments (never
yet compiled in one Tract) reselled and
answered, many Texts of Scripture cleared,
the Quintessence and Marrow of most of
our Modern Authors (in reference to this
Controversie) collected, with References to
such Authors as clear any Doubt more
fully; many incident Cases resolved, the
utmost extent of Lay-mens using their Gifts
in Eleven Particulars demonstrated, and
above Thirty Objections answered.

" In the close are added Six Arguments,
to prove our Ministers free from Anti-
christianism."

The pamphlet itself is an extremely
vigorous attack upon the Baptists, because

they denied original sin to be in infants, regarded infant baptism as "a childish needless thing, and considered that all gifted persons may preach without ordination." Tedious though it seems to-day, it has remarkable shrewdness, and few works of the time show better how the sects were regarded by the common people, learned or unlearned. It holds a distinctly "liberal view" of episcopal ordination, while strongly asserting its obligation, but its main argument, after the usual athletic manipulation of biblical texts, consists in a manly presentation of the Church's claim to the allegiance of the nation.

"Had it been some years since, when God seemed to have been about to depart from us, when Innovations and Corruptions were breaking in upon us, then to withdraw, then to forsake the Church, (however I dare not avouch it for a work so transcendently meritorious as some conceive of it, yet) I grant it tolerable. But now to do it, now that (as themselves conceive of it) the Church is coming up out of the wilderness, now that she begins to boyl out her scum, now that she begins to be more refined and reformed; now to forsake her, truely this is no small aggravation to this desertion.

" For Mariners at Sea to forsake their ship when she is ready to sink, (though possibly it may be an errour and over-sight in them so to do, yet) it is pardonable. But if the ship shall begin to rise and float again, so as they see apparent hopes that with a little pumping and baling she may be saved, now to leave her (much more to cut holes in her sides) their owners will give them little thanks for it. Some yeers since, the Church of God amongst us seemed to be in a sinking condition; then to leave her might be pardonable. But now, now that through the mercy of God she begins to be somewhat floatsome and buoyant, so as a little industry and pains in the pumping and purging may free her and save her, shall we now desert her? (that I do not say cut holes in her sides). Surely, surely, surely, never was Separation from this

Church so unwarrantable as it is at this
day : warrantable it never was since she
was a true Church." *

To such appeals the sectaries turned a
deaf ear. In 1651 and 1652 there were
replies in a very angry vein by Thomas
Collier : " Pulpit Guard Routed, or a brief
answer to a large and lawless Discourse by
one Thomas Hall," and " Pulpit-Guard and
Font-Guard Routed."

It was into a hornet's nest indeed that
Bunyan was come when he was desired to
be a minister. And this ministry was to
be among the Baptists, who were still
thought by many to be tainted with the
vices of John of Leyden and the zealots of
Münster.

The modern Baptist movement had little,
if anything, in common with the German
enthusiasts. Its origin was in Amsterdam.
It broke away from Brownism in 1612. It
had published in 1617 a Declaration of
Faith. Of Baptism it said, " That every

* " The Pulpit Guarded," etc., pp. 69–70.

church is to receive in all their members by
baptism upon the confession of their faith
and sins, wrought by the preaching of the
Gospel according to the primitive institution and practice. And therefore churches
constituted after any other manner, or of
any other person, are not according to
Christ's testament. That baptism or washing with water is the outward manifestation
of dying to sin and walking in newness of
life; and therefore in no wise appertaineth
to infants." It is difficult to be sure that
this declaration would have been, or was,
cordially accepted by Bunyan.

From an early period the Baptists were
subject to fissure. The London Baptists
adopted a Calvinistic Confession (1596) in
1644, whereas the body founded in 1612
was Arminian, and in 1654 it had definite
organisations and a general assembly, the
Calvinistic Baptists adopted a revision of
the Westminster Confession. The others
became less and less clear on the Divinity
of Christ, but their creed was eclectic rather

than Arian or Socinian.* Bunyan, it is clear, belonged to the Calvinist section. He was, in his belief in the Incarnation, orthodox to the core.

In the years before he formally joined the body, English Baptists had gone through a tempest of criticism. In 1645 appeared that highly entertaining tractate, with illustrations of all the types, which bore the title of

" The Dippers dipt. Or, The Anabaptists ducked and plunged Over Head and Eares, at a Disputation in Southwark. Together with A large and full Discourse of

	1.	Originall.
	2.	Severall sorts.
	3.	Peculiar Errours.
Their	4.	High Attempts against the State.
	5.	Capitall punishments : with an Application to these times."

* See *Transactions* of the Baptist Historical Society, Vol. V. No. 3, pp. 172–4.

It is a powerful argument for orthodox ways, as crabbed as cogent. Texts could be freely thrown at Anabaptist heads; as freely as at the Bench of Bishops, and quite as unprofitably. But Dr. Featley had some sense of fun, as when he compared the lures of his opponents with the manner of taking apes in the Indies. So at last he protested that

" . . . These late Proselytes, who invade many empty Pulpits in the City and Sur-burbs, at the first in their Sermons set before thee as it were a Bason of the pure water of life, wherein thou maist see thy face, & wash away the spots of thy Soul; but after they have got thy liking and good opinion, & confide in thee, then they mingle bird-lime with the water of life: the bird-lime of Socinianisme, of Libertinisme, or Antinominianisme, Brownisme, and Ana-baptisme: wherewith, after they have put out or closed the eyes of thy judgement, they lead thee whither they list, and make a prey of thee."

Featley died in 1645 : but controversy was far from dying with him.

Historical information as to the discipline and organisation of the Baptist Society during the reign of Charles II is gradually being accumulated. We have the reports of a spy in 1682 who reports that in the district round London (not the city itself) there were thirteen Baptist ministers and 4250 adherents. Two sections of these, of 300 and 600 men, were still named Fifth Monarchy men. A church in south London dates from 1673. A congregation which assembled in Thames Street, but was gathered from a wide area, shows in the ten years from 1689 but few serious lapses. The rift between the Baptists and the National Church showed no sign of diminution when persecution ceased. Even as late as 1743 the Baptist Board unanimously decided " that it is absolutely unlawful for any member of a Gospel Church to commune with the Church of England on any

consideration whatever." Is this decision
still regarded as valid, one wonders? Certainly it would not have been approved by
Bunyan, though sometimes he seems to
write bitterly of the Church of England. Of
himself he says :

" Since you would know by what name
I would be distinguished from others, I tell
you, I would be, and hope I am, a Christian ;
and chuse, if God should count me worthy,
to be called a Christian, a Believer, or other
such name which is approved by the Holy
Ghost. And as for those factious titles of
Anabaptists, Independents, Presbyterians,
or the like, I conclude that they come
neither from Jerusalem nor from Antioch,
but rather from Hell and Babylon; for
they naturally tend to divisions. You may
know them by their fruits."

Of the orthodoxy of the main beliefs of
Bunyan according to Catholic standards
there can be no doubt. For example, in
" Some Gospel Truths Opened " he vehe-

F

mently asserts " that Christ the Son of the
Virgin is the true God." Organisation, one
feels, seemed to him but a triviality. The
love of God and the revelation of Jesus
Christ were all in all, all that mattered.
Through them alone was the way to heaven.

In the Holy Sacrament Bunyan had a
most touching belief. He must no doubt
have communicated in his youth with the
Church, and knelt at the altar in the
ancient church of Elstow; but when he
" did join in fellowship with the people of
God in Bedford "—and one may conclude
that he means the Baptists—he desired to
" walk in the order and ordinances of Christ
with them," and especially that ordinance
" which was his last supper with his disciples." He then found himself terribly
tempted to blaspheme; and for three-
quarters of a year had no rest or ease, till
at length the converting word came to
him again, and he tells that he became
well and comfortable in partaking, and

" therein discerned the Lord's body, as broken for my sins, and that his precious blood hath been shed for my transgressions."

When we consider Bunyan's adherence, not perhaps particularly close, to the Baptist body, it is well to note that the most recent theological opinion is inclined to put the case more strongly on behalf of that sect than the Church has hitherto been ready to allow. Dr. N. P. Williams in his Bampton Lectures on " The Fall and Original Sin " * says that the custom of baptising infants seems to have grown up from popular feeling rather than from traditional faith.

" It will be clear from this account of the original institution of baptism that the custom of baptising unconscious infants, which, as we have suggested, seems to have grown up spontaneously on a basis of popular feeling, and not of any reasoned theory, and which has now for many

* Pp. 550, *sqq.*

centuries been the normal means of entrance to the Christian Church, involves two very serious difficulties : (1) the apparent incongruity of administering a sacrament, the purpose of which is declared both by its symbolism and by the language of Scripture to be the ' washing away of sins,' to beings who *ex hypothesi* cannot have committed any sins; (2) the exclusive emphasis which the practice appears to lay upon the *opus operatum*, in view of the presumption that unconscious infants are incapable of repentance or of personal faith in Christ. It might in fact be contended, that if the epithets ' magical ' and ' mechanical ' can be applied to any parts of the traditional sacramental system at all, it is the custom of infant baptism first and foremost to which they ought to be affixed; and such a contention might be thought to derive some force from the curious stratagems employed by the Jesuit missionaries in North America to enable them to baptise dying infants amongst the heathen surreptitiously (by unobservedly flicking a few drops of water over the infant's face, and simultaneously whispering *ego te baptizo*, etc., whilst apparently engaged in conversation with the parents), for the purpose of adding as many souls as possible to the Kingdom of God."

As Dr. Williams considers—and no doubt this will now be very generally admitted—that the idea of " original guilt " is no part of the body of revealed Christian truth, it seems to him that the practice of infant baptism must be defended as based upon the decisions and practice of the Catholic Church, and that :

" we neither affirm nor deny the legitimacy of infant baptism, which is a collateral development from the original idea and institution of baptism, and which depends for its authority not upon any credal or conciliar formula, but upon the actual practice of the Church and the semi-articulate instincts of the general body of Christendom."

The Church, however, has certainly never

considered that the legitimacy, as apart from the necessity, of infant baptism could be regarded as an open question.

Bunyan, whether far from or near to the doctrine of the Catholic Church, yet had a grave dislike of some at least of the sects.

Let us take two which seemed to be extremist : the Ranter and the Quaker. In his dislike of the Ranters—and undoubtedly he was a good hater—Bunyan was in full agreement with Baxter, who writes :

" They made it their business to set up the light of Nature, under the name of Christ in men, and to dishonour and cry down the Church, the Scripture, the present Ministry, and our worship and ordinances—and called men to hearken to Christ within them. But withal, they conjoined a cursed doctrine of libertinism, which brought them to all abominable filthiness of life. They taught as the *Familists*, that God regarded not the actions of the outward man, but of the heart." *

* Sylvester's " Life of Baxter," lib. I, p. 76.

The Puritan was in the days of Cromwell and Charles II no more favourably disposed towards the Society of Friends than was the Churchman. Thus Bunyan writes :

" The errors that this people then maintained were : (1) That the Holy Scriptures were not the word of God. (2) That every man in the world had the Spirit of Christ, grace, faith, etc. (3) That Christ Jesus, as crucified and dying sixteen hundred years ago, did not satisfy divine justice for the sins of the people. (4) That Christ's flesh and blood was within the saints. (5) That the bodies of the good and the bad that are buried in the churchyard shall not arise again. (6) That the resurrection is past with good men already. (7) That that man Jesus, that was crucified between two thieves on Mount Calvary, in the land of Canaan, by Jerusalem, was not ascended above the starry heavens. (8) That he should not, even the same Jesus that died by the hand of the Jews, come again at the last day, and as man judge all nations, etc."*

* " The Complete Works of John Bunyan," Vol. I, p. 18.

It may be that Bunyan made exceptions which Baxter would not have made, but the former's general position could hardly be better expressed than in words of the latter :

" The Reformed Churches called Protestants are a party indeed, but deserve not the name of a sect ; for their religion is nothing but simple *Christianity*, protesting against the papal corruptions ; though their minuter differences have made some called Lutherans, some Calvinists, some Episcopal, some Presbyterians, some Independents, and some Politicians or Erastians, to say nothing of Anabaptists (who as they differ only in the point of infant Baptism would have been tolerated by such as Tertullian and Gregory Nazianzene, who persuaded the delay of Baptism ; and by the primitive Churches, which for many hundred years, left all to their liberty, when to be baptized ; and stayed till they sought it)." *

* " Tractate printed by F. J. Powicke. Richard Baxter, ' Under the Cross,' 1662–1691," p. 277.

But the opinions of Bunyan and Baxter were not those of the Rebellion Government.

It has sometimes been supposed that religious toleration was given by Oliver Cromwell, or secured under his rule. This is, of course, not true. Not only was it penal to use, or to attend, the Prayer Book Services—John Evelyn and a congregation of Church-folk were arrested as they were engaged in the service of Holy Communion on Christmas Day; but Socinians were excluded from toleration, and a Romanist was executed, "merely for being a priest," * after appeals had been made in vain to Cromwell to spare his life. The Baptists, or Anabaptists, were, it seems, not free from suspicion of plans for insurrection against the Government, but no doubt because even the most suspicious surveillance does not easily discover who has been baptised and who not, and because

* S. R. Gardiner, " History of the Commonwealth Protectorate," Vol. III. p. 50.

the religious meetings of all " dissenting " bodies were in many respects similar, active measures were not often taken against their worship or beliefs. Till Cromwell's death Bunyan was not free to preach when and where he would, for Cromwellian toleration did not always include the Baptists or Bunyan himself. The records of his church at Bedford show that in March 1658 prayers were being offered for counsel what to do with respect to the indictment against Brother Bunyan at the Assizes for preaching at Easton. There is also a story of his preaching in a country church, perhaps Melbourn, when a Cambridge scholar, riding by and wondering at the concourse of the people, was told that there was one Bunyan, a tinker, preaching. If he went to scoff, he certainly remained to pray, for he became later on a preacher himself. Another tale is that when another Cambridge man reproved him for preaching with no scholar's know-

ledge of the Bible, Bunyan replied that he
believed " the English Bible to be a true
copy also." He was as far indeed from the
ancient tongues as from any revised version.

Another tale of his ministry survives :
it is of an encounter with Thomas Smith,
who, after the manner of those days, held
a great many other preferments together
with the office of librarian of the University
Library at Cambridge. Smith reproached
him for declaring that most of his hearers
were unbelievers. Bunyan was ever ready
to engage in text-flinging, and so there was
a pretty dispute. What right had he to
preach, except he were sent ? Why, the
congregation at Bedford had sent him.
And Smith suitably replied that lay folk
could send only those who had no more
power than themselves to admit to the
sacred ministry of Christ's Church. Smith
continued the controversy in a pamphlet,
" A letter to Mr. E. of Taft, four miles from
Cambridge," in which he denounced the false

doctrine of "the wandering tinker preacher," who intruded into pulpits and caused folk to hate their lawful minister. Violence of action, he asserts, was the companion of violence of tongue : church doors were broken open in order that Bunyan's boisterous tongue might find an audience. Bunyan had, of course, a defender : Henry Denne, also of Cambridge, who declared that Smith was angry with the tinker because he strove to mend souls as well as kettles and pans. There was a sharp controversy on the immemorial lines, or rather on those which have continued since Bugenhagen set at nought the immemorial rule of Apostolic Succession.

But, preach what Bunyan would, he delivered what it is the fashion nowadays to call his "message" with sincerity and emphasis. He tells the story of his beginnings :

" And now I am speaking my experience, I will in this place thrust in a word or two concerning my preaching the word, and of

God's dealing with me in that particular
also; for after I had been about five or six
years awakened, and helped myself to see
both the want and worth of Jesus Christ
our Lord, and also enabled to venture my
soul upon him; some of the most able
among the saints with us, I say, the most
able for judgment and holiness of life, as
they conceived. I did perceive that God
had counted me worthy to understand
something of his will in his holy and blessed
word, and had given me utterance, in
some measure, to express what I saw to
others for edification; therefore they desired
me, and that with much earnestness, that I
would be willing at some times to take in
hand, in one of the meetings, to speak a
word of exhortation unto them.

" The which, though at the first it did
much dash and abash my spirit, yet being
still by them desired and entreated, I
consented to their request, and did twice
at two several assemblies, but in private,
though with much weakness and infirmity,
discover my gift amongst them; at which
they not only seemed to be, but did solemnly

protest, as in the sight of the great God, they were both affected and comforted, and gave thanks to the Father of mercies for the grace bestowed on me.

"After this, sometimes, when some of them did go into the country to teach, they would also that I should go with them; where, though as yet I did not, nor durst not, make use of my gift in an open way, yet more privately still, as I came amongst the good people in those places, I did sometimes speak a word of admonition unto them also; the which they as the other, received with rejoicing at the mercy of God to me-ward, professing their souls were edified thereby.

"Wherefore, to be brief, at last, being still desired by the church, after some solemn prayer to the Lord, with fasting, I was more particularly called forth, and appointed to a more ordinary public preaching the word, not only to and amongst them that believed, but also to offer the gospel to those who had not yet received the faith thereof. About which time I did evidently find in my mind a secret pricking forward thereto: though, I bless

God, not for desire of vain-glory, for at that time I was most sorely afflicted with the fiery darts of the devil concerning my eternal state." *

One would think that the character of the man would make his preaching not only full of fire but also of assurance—and that not in the seventeenth-century theological sense, but rather in that of self-assurance. Yet it may not have been so, or at least not always. At any rate the chief note was pure sincerity. The words that follow have an unmistakable ring of reality about them :

" Indeed I have been as one sent to them from the dead; I went myself in chains, to preach to them in chains; and carried that fire in my own conscience, that I persuaded them to beware of. I can truly say, and that without dissembling, that when I have been to preach, I have gone full of guilt and terror, even to the pulpit

* " The Complete Works of John Bunyan," Vol. I. p. 35.

door, and there it hath been taken off, and I have been at liberty in my mind until I have done my work; and then immediately, even before I could get down the pulpit stairs, I have been as bad as I was before; yet God carried me on, but surely with a strong hand, for neither guilt nor hell could take me off my work.

" Thus I went for the space of two years, crying out against men's sins, and their fearful state because of them. After which the Lord came in upon my own soul with some staid peace and comfort through Christ; for he did give me many sweet discoveries of his blessed grace through him. Wherefore now I altered in my preaching (for still I preached what I saw and felt); now therefore I did much labour to hold forth Jesus Christ in all his offices, relations, and benefits unto the world, and did strive also to discover, to condemn, and remove those false supports and props on which the world doth both lean, and by them fall and perish."*

* " The Complete Works of John Bunyan," Vol. I. p. 36.

Of Bunyan's sermons it is probable that we have many specimens. The great mass of his tracts doubtless had sermons of his for their originals. The sharp phrases with which they are sprinkled are no doubt the vivid words which came readily from his mouth. He would not surrender some of the promises of Christ " for as much gold and silver as can lie between York and London piled up to the stars," while some would far rather have the tales of the Beves of Southampton or S. George and the Dragon than the Bible. Again and again there comes a phrase reminiscent of Shakespeare or of the Elizabethan dramatists. Death "is only a passage out of a sea of trouble into a haven of rest," our Lord " became poorer than they that go with flail and rake."

The form of service, as well as of sermon, may well have been indifferent to him. Just as he would speak from his heart, so would he, with the Church he served, expect every

G

newcomer to the body " to give an account
of the work of grace in his soul."

So we find him first a Baptist, and then a
Baptist preacher; the first probably from
1651, the second from about 1655. From
then till November 12, 1660, when he was
arrested for preaching at Samwell, the
record of his work is meagre. No doubt
he continued his trade : certainly he still
suffered from divers temptations; but
still he went steadily on. It was in these
years, no doubt, that he made that store
of knowledge concerning human desires
and frailties and their outward expression
which is the great characteristic of his
literary work.

The shrewd observation of life and
manners which makes one of the greatest
charms of " The Pilgrim's Progress " is
seen in almost everything that he writes, and
especially, of course, in his autobiographical
reminiscences. When he saw good men
kissing the other sex, he asked them " why

they did salute the most handsome and let
the ill-favoured go?" No defects in human
nature escaped his sharp eye: least of all
his own.

And this displayed itself in his preachings:

"This part of my work," says he, "I
fulfilled with great sense; for the terrors
of the law, and guilt for my transgressions,
lay heavy upon my conscience. I preached
what I felt,—what I smartingly did feel,
—even that under which my poor soul did
groan and tremble to astonishment."

As to the details of his life during the
period 1655 to 1660, which he told in "Grace
Abounding to the Chief of Sinners," first
published in 1666, he was, as Dr. Brown
says, "provokingly reticent." * We must
make out what we can from a few scraps of
fact or feeling and that book. His ministry
was not all happiness, at any rate among
them that are without. There were

* "Life," i. 93.

rumours, he tells us, that he was "a Witch, a
Jesuite, a Highwayman and the like." This
is nothing uncommon in the lives of religious
worthies. Shakespeare described Joan of
Arc as a witch, scores of his contemporaries
believed John Wesley to be a Jesuit, and
one of the long line of Archbishops of York
is still persistently reported to have been a
highwayman—and, some add, to have had
Dick Turpin for his major-domo.

For his spiritual progress we must look
to the words in which he has told us of
his soul and his work. For his temporal
doings we must search among the Bedford
survivals of old days. No doubt he was
more at ease in the town than in the
inquisitive circle of a country village ; but
Bedford was not then what it is now.
Most of the old buildings except the
churches already mentioned * have disappeared : even the old bridge, where it
was long supposed that he wrote "The

* See above, pp. 25 *sqq.*

Pilgrim's Progress" when he was imprisoned in the town lock-up, has gone, and so has the county gaol in Silver Street, where he certainly was confined earlier, when the book was mostly written. In some respects police regulations were much as they have again become in the last few years—a stranger could not be given shelter without recording his name, nationality and ordinary dwelling-place, for the satisfaction of the local authorities. The streets were vigilantly watched by Dogberry and Verges; and yet they were little better to walk in than those Hans Andersen describes in "The Goloshes of Fortune." There was some attempt to illuminate, but in most cases, surely, the light that was in them was darkness.

Ecclesiastical changes in the town seem to have passed almost unobserved, and there is no complaint of persecution. When Gifford died there was a dispute about the appointment to the Rectory and Hospital of S. John, which Cromwell himself decided, but of "the late Rector thereof," Mr. Theodore Crowley—whom John Gifford presumably had replaced—there is no mention in Walker's "Sufferings of the Clergy." The congregation kept records which are still preserved and not uninteresting. They show some little concern in national politics, particularly the offer of the kingship, which Cromwell put aside very much in the manner of Cæsar in Shakespeare's play. And the Quakers were coming into conflict with the Puritan majority. Bunyan had his first fight with them, and Edward Burroughs, a notable personage among them, declared that "John Bunnion said the 30th of the 10th month that the Spirit of Christ doth nothing within man as to justification. O horrid blasphemy! Not to be paralleled": a statement which may remain in its original obscurity. Burroughs*

* See Fox's "Diary" (ed. Harvey, 1911) for many references; and Rufus Jones, "Spiritual Reformers of the Sixteenth and Seventeenth Centuries."

was highly approved by Fox himself, and indeed wrote an introduction to his book "The Great Mystery of the Great Whore," published three years after the contest with Bunyan, but does not seem to have had such gentleness or sagacity as would enable him to understand of what spirit was the man so soon to write "The Pilgrim's Progress."

In 1657 the records show Bunyan as appointed to preach on a special occasion.

It has been already mentioned that in 1658 an indictment was preferred against him for preaching at Elstow. As Dr. Brown has pointed out, "religious liberty had not come to mean liberty all round, but only liberty for a certain recognised section," and Precentor Venables, in his introduction to an edition of "The Pilgrim's Progress," reminds us that in Bedfordshire some women Quakers were whipped and sent to Bridewell for reproving a minister and urging people to repentance. It was not merely that new presbyter was but old

priest writ large, but also that the government which patrolled the country with
armed horsemen was not satisfied unless
all English folk were under its heel.

These years then were troublous; round
Bunyan, without were fightings, within
were fears. But for the most part he held
on his way in Bedford steadily, sought after
and beloved.

AND at length the King had his own
again; and, after him, the Church returned
in peace. Englishmen could again say the
Common Prayer and be married in church.
It was not long after the Restoration
before those who resented the preaching of
tinkers lifted up their voices in protest.
Bunyan had been supported by the Master
of Caius and allowed to preach in his church
of Yelden. Parishioners petitioned the
House of Lords, newly restored to its
hereditary dignity, against their academic
rector. He had allowed one Bunyan, a
tinker of Bedford, to speak from the pulpit
on the last Christmas Day, " and no
orthodox minister did officiate in the
church that day." Indeed, as we know
from Evelyn, it was penal to minister the
Holy Communion according to the ancient

rite on that sacred day no less than on others. The petition was dated June 20, 1660, and dismissed on July 25. It was not yet safe to assert the rights of the Church of England. Bunyan still went on preaching and writing. "The Doctrine of the Law and Grace Unfolded" came out in May 1659, a pathetic record, in many respects, of his own spiritual struggles. For a few months he remained in peace.

But those who were now in power, the laity who had lost goods and property during the Commonwealth, and had not been allowed to hear their own ministers, to have their children christened with the old form, or be married in their parish church, were determined to get the power into their own hands again and to have the old laws of good Queen Bess enforced. It was not only the country squires who protested against (or had suffered under, as "The Verney Letters" show) the Cromwellian tyranny. Clergy and men of letters too had learnt the hollowness of the changes which some had accepted and some eulogised. What Milton came to think of "new presbyters" we know, but it is not so often remembered that in his "History of Britain" he came to denounce those who were "pastors in name but in deed wolves," with "intent not to feed the flock but to pamper and well line themselves." The pretended Reform inaugurated by the Westminster Assembly now seemed to him to be a pretence and delusion: statesmen and churchmen alike when in power had been proved unworthy, and the very people had ceased to believe in the religion which such leaders professed.

"Then * they who of late were extolled as our greatest deliverers, and had the people wholly at their devotion, by so discharging their trust as we see, did not only weaken

* Milton, "Character of the Long Parliament," p. 9 (1681). See Firth in *Proceedings of the British Academy*, Vol. 3.

and unfit to be dispensers of what liberty they pretended, but unfitted also the people, now grown worse and more disordinate, to receive or digest any liberty at all. For stories teach us that liberty sought out of season, in a corrupt and degenerate age, brought Rome itself into a further slavery; for liberty hath a sharp and double edge, fit only to be handled by just and virtuous men; to bad and dissolute, it becomes a mischief unwieldy in their own hands: neither is it completely given, but by them who have the happy skill to know what is grievous and unjust to a people, and how to remove it wisely; what good laws are wanting, and how to frame them substantially, that good men may enjoy the freedom which they merit, and the bad the curb which they need. But to do this, and to know the exquisite proportions, the heroic wisdom which is required surmounted far the principles of these narrow politicians: what wonder then if they sunk these unfortunate Britons before them, entangled and oppressed with things too hard and generous above their strain and temper?"

Milton knew that liberty, to be true liberty, must be disciplined by virtue: as a century later the liberty that Burke advocated was a liberty connected with order. No one felt that there had been either a secure or a just Government since the Long Parliament began. " Malignants " and " prelatists " alike now clamoured for justice. The squires demanded their estates, and in still greater numbers the clergy their livings, of which they had been deprived because they refused to accept the new ecclesiastical government that had been thrust upon them. In September 1660 the " formerly ejected or sequestered ministers " were restored to their benefices by law. The reaction was felt all over England. Even Puritan Bedfordshire expressed it. The Quarter Sessions, while Parliament was not sitting, anticipated events by ordering the public reading of the Liturgy of the Church of England. It is noted that William Annand, still a famous

name among clergy of Northants and Beds.,
preached in favour of the return to the old
service. When the great Sanderson came
as Bishop of Lincoln before the end of the
year to Bedford he was received with
military and civil as well as ecclesiastical
rejoicing.* But all the old ways could not
be re-established, the Bedfordshire folk felt,
without recourse to the old laws. The
statute 1 Eliz c. 2, which was supplemented
by other Elizabethan laws, and was re-
enacted by Charles II, required all persons
to resort to church every Sunday, and her
Conventicle Act (35 Eliz c. 6) made fre-
quenting such assemblies punishable by
imprisonment. On November 12, 1660,
John Bunyan was to preach at Samwell,
about thirteen miles south of Bedford. He
was warned, but he persisted. When he

* Dr. Brown, in his most excellent " Life of
Bunyan," Vol. I. p. 30, quaintly remarked that the
sounds must have reached the ears of " another
Bishop " : he means Bunyan, who really never claimed
even the priesthood, still less the episcopate.

approached the farm-house where he was
to preach he was warned again, and he still
persevered. He opened his Bible : he
prayed : and then came a constable and a
man from Mr. Wingate, a local magistrate,
who had issued a warrant for his arrest.
Bunyan addressed his congregation as men
of his opinion generally did : they were
doing Christ's work ; they were persecuted
for doing good; what was said about the
law was of less moment. So he wrote later :

" Having made profession of the glorious
gospel of Christ a long time, and preached
the same about five years, I was appre-
hended at a meeting of good people in the
country, (among whom, had they let me
alone, I should have preached that day,
but they took me away from amongst
them,) and had me before a justice ; who
after I had offered security for my appearing at the next sessions, yet committed me,
because my sureties would not consent to
be bound that I should preach no more to
the people.

" At the sessions after I was indicted for
an upholder and maintainer of unlawful
assemblies and conventicles, and for not
conforming to the national worship of the
Church of England; and after some con-
ference there with the justices, they taking
my plain dealing with them for a confession,
as they termed it, of the indictment, did
sentence me to a perpetual banishment,
because I refused to conform. So being
again delivered up to the gaoler's hands,
I was had home to prison, and there have
lain now complete twelve years, waiting
to see what God would suffer these men to
do with me." *

What happened was that on his arrest
the magistrate who had issued the warrant
was discovered to be away from home;
and a friend became Bunyan's bail that he
should appear next day. When that came
the Justice, Mr. Francis Wingate at Harling-
ton, asked what had been done. He found,

* " The Complete Works of John Bunyan," Vol. I.
pp. 39–40.

of course, that it was not a seditious
but only an illegal gathering. Evidently
(Bunyan thinks) he would have dismissed
the case, had not the preacher persisted in
his assertion that he must preach the
" word." He offered to take sureties that
the preaching should not continue. But
this Bunyan would not allow. " I should
not leave speaking the word of God ; even
to counsel, comfort, exhort and teach the
persons among whom I came." It sounded
innocent enough, and so, no doubt, it was,
for Bunyan was no fanatical politician,
and was in favour, it seems, of the Restoration. But magistrates have to administer the
law : and country squires at that time were
writhing under the memory of persecution
and the irritation of being preached to
(or at) by ill-educated folk. There was a
real political danger to the restored monarchy : the first few months of the reign
showed it. And the country folk could
not get out of their heads that it was the

H

unlicensed preachers, who departed from
the old ways and put forth what seemed a
new individual gospel, and the sects which
were without recognised root and branch,
who were at the back of all the troubles of
the last twenty years. There came in,
while Justice and prisoner were engaged
in a not unfriendly but rather irritating
conversation, the vicar of the parish, who
would seem, according to Bunyan's report,
to have been a somewhat pompous person.
Bunyan rather insolently replied to him
that he did not come there to talk to him
but to the Justice, at which Mr. Lindell
made an impolite allusion to Alexander
the coppersmith, and soon each began to
taunt the other with Pharisaism.

Wingate may have been influenced by
the harsh treatment—unjust certainly, if
not at the moment illegal—to which he and
his mother had been subject during the war.
But he did not go beyond the letter of the
law : he would break the neck of these

meetings, he said; and Bunyan (one wonders in what tone) replied that "it might be so."

So he was committed to Bedford Gaol—the county gaol it must have been. Yet even then he was given a further chance, which a lawyer, Foster, afterwards Chancellor of the diocese of Lincoln, urged him to accept. Would he promise not to call the people together? The Justice was very loth to send him to prison if he would but be ruled. Again an irritating talk. Bunyan stood quite firm to his duty to preach: the others could not see why that should not be left to the lawful ministry. No one indeed in that time of disordered thought and life was willing to allow those who disagreed with government in Church or State to have any "liberty of prophesying." Cromwell had not allowed the Church to have its prayers: why should Charles allow the sects to have their preachings?

So Bunyan went to prison, and after he

had been there nearly a week another attempt was made to relese him on bail. But the magistrate appealed to, after hesitation, did not see how it could be done. Nor indeed could it be, if the object was to prevent the gathering of the people together, which Bunyan would certainly not consent to do. And Bunyan hoped that his imprisonment might lead to " an awakening to the Saints in the country." Ill-omened phrase : men were sick of the rule of " the Saints," and the last thing they desired was to stir them to activity again. There seems to have been no ill-feeling against Bunyan; indeed Foster made as though he would have kissed him, which Bunyan considered to be hypocritical, though that seems extraordinarily unlikely. Indeed, Bunyan as a man seems to have been, as one might fancy from the cheery tone of his most famous books, a popular personage. Hardly ever do his enemies (except the opposing sect) throw a hard word at him.

When the Quarter Sessions came on, in January 1661, he was brought before the magistrates. It was a bench above the average of intelligence, and certainly no more prejudiced than men of either party were in those days. Sir John Keeling was a barrister, but he had spent almost all the interregnum in gaol. He rose rapidly when the King came home, and by 1665 was Lord Chief Justice of England. Among the others, Sir George Blundell had suffered severely in pocket during the Cromwellian tyranny. Another became sheriff. The indictment was for " devilishly and per- niciously abstaining from coming to church to hear divine service, and for being a common upholder of several unlawful meet- ings and conventicles, with great dis- turbance and distraction of the good sub- jects of this kingdom, contrary to the laws of our sovereign lord the King": a riot of words such as lawyers have always enjoyed. When questioned, Bunyan quibbled by saying he did go to the Church of God.

Keeling pulled him up sharply : " Do you come to church ?—You know what I mean, to the parish church, to hear divine service ? " No, of course. Why? Because it was not commanded in the Word of God to pray by the Book of Common Prayer. Bunyan did not think the Book of Common Prayer, but only the Spirit, could teach men to pray. But why, no doubt the magistrates were thinking, could not a man pray with the Spirit and with the understanding also ? Keeling seems to have questioned most patiently. Bunyan's retort always came to the same point : it was " not commanded in the Word of God." It is the old argument which Hooker against Cartwright had long ago demolished. Then he would prove (" as every man hath received the gift ") that it was his duty not only to pray but to preach. At last the wrangle—for really it was little better, although conducted with good temper on both sides—ended, for Keeling saw it would never end unless he stopped it.

The decision of Keeling was clear, and became important. It was that as Bunyan would persist in a lengthy disquisition and not give a plain or concise answer, he must be regarded as having practically confessed. Here Keeling believed that he was following the great Bracton. And so Bunyan was convicted under the Elizabethan Conventicle Act, made permanent since 1624 and never repealed.

Bunyan in his Relation of his imprisonment, published in 1665, writes thus :

" Then, said he, hear your judgment. You must be had back again to prison, and there lie for three months following; and at three months' end, if you do not submit to go to church to hear Divine service, and leave your preaching, you must be banished the realm : and if, after such a day as shall be appointed you to be gone, you shall be found in this realm, &c., or be found to come over again without special licence from the king, &c., you must stretch by the neck for it, I tell you plainly; and so he bid my jailor have me away.

" *Bun.* I told him, as to this matter, I was at a point with him; for if I was out of prison to-day I would preach the gospel again to-morrow, by the help of God.

" *Another.* To which one made me some answer; but my jailor pulling me away to be gone, I could not tell what he said.

" Thus I departed from them; and I can truly say, I bless the Lord *Jesus Christ* for it, that my heart was sweetly refreshed in the time of my examination, and also afterwards, at my returning to the prison. So that I found *Christ's* words more than bare trifles, where he saith, He will give a mouth and wisdom, even such as all the adversaries shall not gainsay or resist. And that his peace no man can take from us.

" Thus have I given you the substance of my examination. The Lord make these profitable to all that shall read or hear them. Farewell."

" So," he says, " being again delivered up to the gaoler's hands, I was had home to prison again." He was there visited by Cobb, Clerk of the Peace, who put the demand of the law plainly before him.

There was reason for enforcing it, for the Fifth Monarchy and various old Cromwellians had already begun to raise their armed heads again. Cobb and Bunyan argued about these matters and their possible connection with unlicensed religious meetings. Cobb showed what a pity it would be if Bunyan had to be banished. Bunyan replied by an assertion of what came to be a famous doctrine, that of passive obedience. As to the legal point, it is most clearly put by Dr. Brown, whom I will quote.*

" Bunyan had been convicted under the unrepealed Conventicle Act of 1593, and all persons so convicted were committed to prison, ' there to remain without bail or mainprise, until they shall conform and yield themselves to come to some church, chapel, or usual place of common prayer and hear divine service and make such open submission and declaration of their said conformity ' as the Act requires. The submission was to be made publicly and at

* " Life," Vol. I. p. 147.

service-time, before the sermon or reading
of the gospel. It was then by the minister
to be entered into a book to be kept in
every parish for the purpose and within ten
days certified to the bishop in writing. If
the convicted person did not make this
submission within three months he shall
'abjure this realm of England and all
other the Queen's Majesty's dominions for
ever.' Three months' confinement had
done nothing to subdue the spirit of this
resolute prisoner. He still held to his
purpose, and still defended their meetings,
the object of which he said was simply to
do each other as much good as they could
according to their light, and not to disturb
the peace of the nation."

Cobb's was an official visit, to explain
that if the prisoner did not conform within
three months he must abjure the realm.
Bunyan was required to appear at the
Quarter Sessions on April 13 to make oath
of submission or suffer the consequences.
But this was postponed because of the wide
pardon expected to be proclaimed at the

King's coronation, and on April 25 actually given. To take advantage of this the prisoner was required to sue for a pardon. Bunyan did not do so, but sent his wife to London for advice to " Lord Barkwood." *
He was referred to the Judge of Assize.

Bunyan then stayed in prison till August, when came the Midsummer Assizes. Now his excellent wife came forward on his behalf. Bunyan is very reticent about his marriages. His first wife died about the same time as John Gifford. When did he marry his second wife? Apparently a year or so before his arrest at Samwell. Slanderous tongues accused him of having two wives: there is no excuse that we know of for such a malicious charge. Of the first wife we know practically nothing : of the second, her devotion and courage.

It had been hoped that the pardons

* Who was " Lord Barkwood " ? He was not a peer, nor one of Cromwell's House of Lords. Neither the Hon. Vicary Gibbs nor Sir Charles Frith can identify him. Perhaps a judge, thus loosely entitled by Mrs. Bunyan.

granted at the coronation of Charles II
might include him; but they did not. So,
determined, as he says, "not to leave any
possible means unattempted that might be
lawful," he caused his wife thrice to present
his petition to the Justices of Assize. The
first who received it was the famous Sir
Matthew Hale, who said he would "do the
best good he could" for wife and husband.
Next day a petition was thrown into
Justice Twisdon's coach, who sharply
answered that being convicted he could
not be released without promise of submission to the law. So too said Justice
Chester on the request being repeated
when Hale and he were in court.

Mrs. Bunyan received encouragement
from the High Sheriff, and so tried
again. In fact everyone wished to do the
best for the good man, but the law was
the law, though the tinkers may have
thought it an ass. A final interview,
recorded at great length by Bunyan, who
never when writing about himself used one

word where two would do, took place
between the wife and the Justices when
many Justices and gentry of the county
were present. The wife, after the manner
of her sex, declared the imprisonment to be
unlawful and the indictment false : this
she repeated again and again, though Judge
Twisdon, after the manner of his kind,
replied, " Do you think we can do what we
list ? Your husband is convicted by the
law." The woman would not be silenced :
the judges would not repudiate the law.
But Hale was compassionate and asked her
gently about her condition, her age, her
marriage, her children and step-children,
and told her that there were only three
things that could be done : appeal to the
King, or sue out a writ of pardon, or get a
writ of error. The poor woman thought
that Justice Chester was " in a chafe " at
this, and scratched his head for anger—no
necessary explanation of such an act in a
stuffy room during a hot August. So she
left the room in tears. And the Justices

must answer for what they have done in the body. And the Statute Book was brought. And what they said of it, Bunyan knew not, nor apparently cared, for his conscience was above statutes. But the law of the matter was perfectly plain.

So the following legal statement shows :—

" Imprisoned till Conformity, 1660.

" One Bunyon was indicted upon the Statute of 35 Elizabeth, for being at a Conventicle. He was in prison, and was brought into Court and the indictment read to him; and because he refused to plead to it, the Court ordered me to record his confession, and he hath lain in prison upon that conviction, ever since Christmas Sessions, 12 Chas. II. And my Lord Chief Justice Keelinge was then upon the Bench, and gave the rule, and had the like, a year ago, against others. Bunyon hath petitioned all the Judges of Assize, as they came the Circuit, but could never be released. And truly, I think it but reasonable that if any one do appear, and afterwards will not plead, but that you should take judgment by *nihil dicit*, or confession." *

Bunyan seems to have been now treated with great leniency. He was released from prison from time to time. He is known to have preached in September and October and to have gone to London. But he did not sue out his pardon or apply, as Sir Matthew Hale suggested, for a writ of error. He now was put down, certainly by an error, for trial at the March Assizes. But, as Cobb points out, he was already in the position of a convicted prisoner. Recent cases showed the result of applying for a writ of error, and Cobb explained the illegality of now trying Bunyan and the un-wisdom of applying for a writ of error which would probably lead to his imprisonment for life. By a new Conventicle Act, 1664, Keeling's rule, as to silence being taken as a

* Document of Paul Cobb, Clerk of the Peace, first printed in *Transactions of the Baptist Historical Society*, Vol. VI. No. 1, p. 5.

confession, was made law. Bunyan then remained in prison, which was an alternative to a much worse fate.

During his absence his congregation again and again recorded its sorrows. Thus:

" We are agreed to set apart ye 12th of ye next month to seeke the Lord in ye behalfe of the congregation, that God would directe and keepe us in such a time as this; and also for all the churches of God and for ye nation, that he would direct our governors in their meeting together.

" The Church (notwithstanding their sore persecutions now come upon them) having spent many dayes in prayer with fasting, to seeke a right way of the Lord in this matter; did joyntly make choyce of brother Samuel ffenne (now lately delivered out of prison) and brother John Whiteman for their pastors and elders, to minister the word and ordinances of Jesus Christ to them; and they at this meeting did solemnly before God and the Lord Jesus Christ, and the elect angells, give up themselves to serve, feed and watch over this congregation, for Jesus' sake (according to the charge layde upon them and accepted by them) according to the measure of grace received.

" God appearing in his glory to build up Zion, there was with joy received into fellowship with this congregation Jonah Whittimore, Henry Warde, Elizabeth Maxye, Sister Locke, and Joane Layton."*

But it was not only sorrows that were recorded in these minute books. Bitterness of feeling is patent in such passages as those which follow :—

" Bedford, ye 30th day of the 8th moneth. (1668). Many of the friends having in these troublous times with-drawne themselves from close walking with the Church and not being reclaimed by those admonitions, that, as time would serve, had been sent to them formerly, some also being guilty of more grosse miscarriages, the Congregation having kept certaine days

* Quoted in Brown's " John Bunyan, His Life, Times and Work," Vol. I. pp. 194–5.

I

with fasting and prayer, bewailed their fall,
did now agree in a solemne way to renew
their admonitions. And did agree That
brother Samuel ffenne and brother John
ffenne and brother Bunyan should speake
with brother Robert Nelson and admonish
him for his withdrawing from the Church
and other miscarriages. And that brother
Samuel ffenne and brother John Croker go
to our brother Richard Deane, to admonish
him and rebuke him for his withdrawing
from the assemblyes of the saints, and
to inquire into ye truth of those scandalous
reports that we heare concerning him. It
was desired also that brother Bunyan and
brother Harrington send for brother Merrill
and admonish him concerning his withdrawing from the Church and his conformity to ye world's way of worship. And
brother Bunyan and brother Cooper were
appointed to go to brother Coventon to
admonish him and endeavour his conviction
for his sin in withdrawing from the Church
assemblyes.

" At a full assembly of this Congregation,
the 21st day of the 10th moneth : Humphrey

Merrill was cut off from, and cast out of this Church of Christ, ffor—

" 1. Breaking covenant with God and fellowship with this congregation.

" 2. ffor an open recanting his profession at a General Quarter Sessions.

" 3. And rejecting and trampling upon the admonitions and intreaties, and all indeavours of the Church, to recover him to amendment of life : disdainefully returning for their care and indeavours to reclaime him such ungodly railing as these : That they had their hands in the blood of the King : that they were disobedient to government, and that they were not a Church; despising also the gifts of and doctrines of God in the Congregation : together with severall other false and heinous accusations.

" Things laid to ye charge of Richard Deane :

" 1. ffor that he after a very ungodly manner separated himself from this congregation and the word and ordinances of Christ therein.

" 2. He after this lived a loose and ungodly life accompanyed with defrauding in his calling; selling to severall persons deceitfull goodes, to the great scandall of our profession.

" 3. ffor speaking contemptuously of the Church.

" 4. He went in the name of the Church, particularly naming Joh. Bunyan and Sam ffenne, and yet wholly without their knowledge or consent, to beg the charity of ye good people of St. Neots; ffor all which things, and many others, he hath bene admonished, by the space of some years; yet could not be brought to repentance for the same.

" Robert Nelson's practices were as followeth :

" 1. He forsooke the Church with the order of the Gospell therein.

" 2. In a great assembly of the Church of England, he was openly and profanely bishopt after the Anti-christian order of that Generation; to ye great profanation of God's order and heartbreaking of his Christian brethren." *

* " Life of John Bunyan," Vol. I. pp. 198, 199, 200.

Thus the iniquities of poor Richard Nelson seem to have been merely that he went to church, and that he had been confirmed. If it was wicked to be baptised, *a fortiori* it was a blasphemy to be confirmed.

We cannot say that Bunyan was responsible for these arrogant eccentricities. He was doubtless still, nominally at least, in prison. How long then did he actually spend in Bedford County gaol?

For a long time it has been supposed that he was released in 1666. But all the evidence points the other way. There was no Declaration, or Act, of indulgence in that year; and Bunyan had taken no steps to comply with the requirements of the existing law. And the Clerk of the Peace very clearly stated in 1670 that " he hath laid in prison," upon the original conviction, "since the Christmas Session 12 Charles II " (*i.e.* 1660). Dr. Whitley has suggested,* very plausibly, that in the con-

* *Transactions of the Baptist Historical Society,* Vol. I. p. 13 (1918).

fusion caused by the plague in 1666 he may have been released for a time. Certainly he was employed by his church in November 1668 and September and November 1669, and he attended meetings there in January and April 1670.

Indeed throughout the period Bunyan was actively engaged in the work of the Bedford Society. Entries given by Dr. Brown from these records may be quoted to show this. Thus :

" In the latter part of the yeare 1669 our brother Harrington being driven from his family to avoyde being taken with a writ De Ecom. capiend., and other friends having of a long time had their habitation at a distance from us, the Congregation did appoint the Elders in their names to write certaine letters to them for their comfort and edification, the copyes of some of them (which were sent with ye Churches full approbation) being now come to hand are here inserted.

" To our brother Harrington was sent this

following " (from which, as being evidently from Bunyan's hand, some extracts may here be given).

" Dearly beloved brother, Grace, mercy, and peace be with you alwayes. With length of dayes is understanding; your long progresses in the wayes of God and our ffather, hath given you rich experience. Wherefore, brother, make it manifest that you are one of those scribes we read of, not only instructed into but unto the Kingdome of God. Gravity becometh the ancients of the House of God : ffathers should be examples unto children. We are comforted in remembrance of thee, brother, while we consider that, notwithstanding thy naturall infirmity, yet thou prizest good conscience above thine owne injoyments : and since thou couldest not with quiet injoy it at home, thou hast left thy concernes in this world, (though in much hazzard and danger) that thou mayest keep it abroad. But remember that good word of God : no man shall desire thy Land when thou shalt go up to appeare before the Lord thy God, thrice in ye yeare.

Wherefore let neither the remembrance of what thou hast left, nor thought of its being subject to casualty either distract thee in thy communion with God, or prevaile with thee to do aught against good conscience, or unworthy thy gray haires; which are then the glory of old men when found in the way of righteousness.

"You, brother Harrington, have lived to see the slippery and unstable nature that is in earthly things; wherefore we beseech you to expect no more therefrom, then the word of God hath promised, which is as much in little as in much thereof, if not more in many respects. While Israell sate by the fleshpots in Egypt they had no manna from heaven, they dranke not the water out of the Rock. We hope it is because God loveth you that he hath driven you from your incumbrances, that you may have occasion before you dye to solace yourself with your God and the Lord Jesus Christ. We meane that you may doe it with more leisure and lesse distraction than when ye lowing of the oxen had continuall sound in your eares.

" God is wise, and doth all things for the best for them that love him. You know not but you shall know afterwards what sins and temptations God hath prevented by driving you thus from your habitation, and how hereby he made way for the exercise of some graces that could not so well discover themselves in their virtues when you was here. How subject we are to dote upon and to be intangled with the snares that lye couched and hid in the things of this present world, you have had great experience with us. When we are desolate then we trust in God, and make prayers and supplications to him night and day. God help you, therefore, that you spend your vacant houres not as they that wept for Tammuz, but as they who plainely confesse to all they are strangers and pilgrims in the earth. Arm yourself with y t mind you read of, Heb. xii. 2, 3, 4, that you may have your garments alwayes white, and that your head may lack no oyntment. You cannot be there where no eyes are upon you. You are a spectacle to God, Angells, and Men ;

and being exalted to ye profession of
Christianity, and also to the comunion
of God and his saintes, you can neither
stand nor fall by yourself, but the name
and cause and people of God shall in some
sense stand and fall with you. Yea, let
us have joy in thee, brother, refresh our
spirits in the Lord. And remember that
God hath saide, Though there were of you
cast out to the uttermost part of heaven,
yet will I gather them from thence, and
will bring them unto the place that I have
chosen to set my name there.

"ffinally, brother, ffarewell. Grace be
with thee. Amen.

"Written by the appointment of y e
Congregation to which you stand related
in y e faith of the Gospell, and subscribed
with their consent by the hands of your
brethren.

"JOHN WHITEMAN   SAMUEL FFENNE
   JOHN BUNYAN   JOH. FFENNE, &c."*

So, in imprisonment which must have

* Dr. Brown's "Life of Bunyan," Vol. I. pp. 200
sqq.

been irksome though it was not rigorous, Bunyan continued his work, and was a trusted leader among his people. Doubtless he saw his wife and children from time to time, for there was something like an open door in the prisons of that day; and he may sometimes have been able to visit them in Bedford. So time went on.

In May 1670 a new Conventicle Act, much less severe than that of Elizabeth, came into force. But Charles, from the Declaration of Breda, had never shown the slightest sympathy for persecution. It was one of the few points in which he was honest, though he was compelled from time to time to yield to his Parliament, for he did not wish " to go on his travels again." In March 1672 he issued his famous Declaration of Indulgence, which Parliament soon declared to be illegal. At the end of the previous year the Bedford congregation, anticipating or relying upon the instances of the slackness of gaolers, appointed Bunyan their pastor, and he was admitted to office. In March also the King's licence for the use of Josiah Roughed's house for worship was obtained. On this site the Baptist services have been held ever since. In October 1672 the Leicester records show that Bunyan's licence to preach, there inspected, bore date May 15, 1672, and was " to teach in the house of Joseph Roughhed, Bedford, or in any other place, room, or house licensed by his Majesty." He was, as the application shows, to be a " Congregation Teacher." There is a difficulty about the dates, but it is of no serious importance.

Now on May 8, 1672, a petition had been presented to the King, on behalf of Bunyan and others, imprisoned for " being at Conventicles and Nonconformity." The pardon was procured, not later than September 13. On October 6 Bunyan, having shown his licence, preached at

Leicester. But Parliament forced the King to withdraw his declaration : could it force him to withdraw or cancel a licence? No doubt it could do the latter; and consequently, on March 4, 1675, the county magistrates issued a warrant for Bunyan's arrest.

It runs thus :

" To the Constables of Bedford "; and it states that notwithstanding the King's

" clemencie and indulgent grace and favour yett one John Bunnyon of your said towne, Tynker, hath divers times within one month last past in contempt of his Majties good laws preached or teached at a Conventicle meeting or assembly under colour or pretence of exercise of Religion in other manner than according to the Liturgie or Practice of the Church of England. These are therefore in his Majties name to command you forthwith to apprehend and bring the Body of the said John Bunnion beefore us or any of us his Majties Justice of Peace within the said county to answer the premises."

There are the names of thirteen magistrates attached to this warrant. Dr. Brown notes : " Among them was that of Bunyan's old enemy, William Foster, who was probably the main mover in the matter." *

Now, if he were convicted of preaching, the penalty was a fine of £40, without imprisonment. But had Bunyan so much as £40, and was it not desirable to arrest so notorious a leader of Nonconformity ? It seems that, doubtless for one or other of these reasons, resort was had to the civil consequences of ecclesiastical law. Bunyan was undoubtedly excommunicate, for not attending the Church services or having his children baptised. It appears that on this ground he was again imprisoned—tradition says, for six months. It was during this imprisonment that he wrote his " Destruction for the Ignorant " and " The Strait Gate," and at least began " The Pilgrim's Progress,"

* " Life of John Bunyan," Vol. II. p. 3.

which was published in December 1677.
It would seem that this time he was
imprisoned not in the county gaol but in
the city lock-up (which was also partly
a toll-house) standing on the ancient bridge
which spanned the River Ouse. He was
released by an order from Barlow, Bishop
of Lincoln, who had probably been responsible for his last imprisonment. For
the last eight years of his life he was a
free man.

His imprisonment, though there are many
signs that he felt it deeply, and the prisons
in those days were abominable places, was,
as we have seen, not often, if ever, a
rigorous one. There was much freedom
of access to him, and he preached often
outside, and gave spiritual courses within
the walls. But his conscientious objection
to the rules of Church and State remained
firm throughout.

We are so far away, and have had so
little experience in recent times of turbulent

politics inducing a turbulent religion that
it is difficult for us to understand how
dangerous the admixture seemed to the
men who had suffered under the Commonwealth, who had seen Cromwell shoot the
Levellers at Burford, and in whose eyes
the Fifth Monarchy men and the old Iron-
sides were a persistent menace to public
security. Just as Charles did not want to
resume his travels, so the ordinary Englishman did not want to be patrolled by troopers
or preached at by sectaries. And so Church
and State stood together. Bunyan, from
most conscientious motives, would not obey
the laws of either. Everyone sooner or later
finds good reason to break the law; but
the mischief begins when, contrary to New
Testament precedent, he argues for his
action on religious grounds. And this
Bunyan did, one must say most extrava-
gantly, in the discourses he preached in
prison. These show him to have an in-
domitable spirit, but by no means to have

been a martyr to consistency. Christians are praised for standing " everyone in their places " and growing where the gardener planted them. But how about the trade of tinker or " brassyer "? Everybody, you say, was inconsistent. " The right to preach was, in the end, conceded by that power which had spent twelve years in asserting that it did not exist," says Dr. Brown.* Not at all: it was the King who gave Bunyan license to preach, and all that the State had ever said was that the right of public preaching could only be enjoyed by licence of the State. Now that Bunyan enjoyed it, his life proceeded placidly. As he grew old the ties of his youth, which he seems never to have felt to be very close, snapped one by one. His mother, we know, had died when he was a boy. His father lived till 1676, when he was buried at Elstow. He appears never to have left the communion of the Church.

* " Life of John Bunyan," Vol. I. p. 186.

K

He bequeathed to each of his children a shilling, probably as much as he could leave in times when the good Samaritan could only afford twopence to the innkeeper.

Years of peace, if not of leisure, were now devoted to literary composition. Bunyan's fertility was amazing, and the greater part of it belongs to this period. It will be best to treat of it separately in this book, but it may be well here just to say two things. First, the style is generally that which Ben Jonson reprehended in Shakespeare. He seems to have written with a full pen and never to have blotted a line. One is inclined to repeat : " Would he had blotted a thousand." And, secondly, the chief characteristic of all the writings, except the very strictly theological ones, is that they are drawn from the life. Bunyan's Apocalypses are extraordinarily profitable as pictures of life and manners in his day. If he kept his eyes and ears open when he was in prison, much more did he do so in the last years of his life, when he was preaching to multitudes, ministering to sick souls, travelling about the country up and down, in city and village, and watching his fellow citizens too in the rather narrow environment of Bedford. " The Holy War " and " The Life and Death of Mr. Badman " are pictures of what Bunyan saw and heard and did in the last twenty years of his life.

Meanwhile, the way of politicians in Court and country was tangled and precarious. Charles II was astute to the end, and the statesmen who surrounded him had little of the solid if prejudiced honesty of his earliest advisers. Bedford was still a home of " conventicles and phanaticks." Mr. Audley, the Deputy Recorder, who spoke up for Bunyan before the King, and Mr. Cobb, the Clerk of the Peace, come again to the front in the story. The corporation was packed with new burgesses

who were believed to be safe men. The
charter was surrendered to the Crown.
Such things were happening all over the
land. All the while Bunyan's pen was
never laid aside. John Howe, the famous
chaplain of Oliver Cromwell who had protested against the " lewd life " of the
Protector's household, raised his voice in
protest against the coercion of dissenters.
Bunyan prepared for the worst. Anticipating the device of the twentieth century
to protect his property from the Government of his country, he made a deed of
gift of all he possessed to his good wife
Elizabeth. In it he still describes himself
as a " brazier," a designation perhaps more
accurate and certainly more polite than
that of tinker; but whether he still worked
with his hands we know not. Among the
numerous offspring of his literary fever at
this time it is pleasant to find, besides the
too often bitter polemics, that charming
little " Book for Boys and Girls," which

showed that, like all good people, he kept a love of children to the end.

James II's attempts at toleration were from the first suspect, and while, so far as he persecuted anyone, he persecuted the ancient Church of England, whose Seven Bishops stood forth nobly in defence of the law of the land, the freedom which he gave to dissenters was not acceptable to the Protestants among them because it excluded that portion of the separatists which accepted the supremacy of the Pope. A letter, now in the Rawlinson MSS. at the Bodleian, written by the son of one of the founders of Bunyan's congregation, shows very clearly what the dissenting feeling was. It has been doubted, though there seems no reason to doubt, whether it truly represented the opinions of Bunyan himself. It was addressed to Lord Aylesbury :

" My Lord, since your Honour spake with me at Bedford I have conferred with the heads of the Dissenters and particularly

with Mr. Margetts and Mr. Bunyon whom
your Lordship named to me. The first of
these was Judge-Advocate in the Army
under the Lord General Monke, when the
late King was restored; the other is Pastor
of the Dissenting congregation in this
Town. I find them all to be unanimous for
electing only such Members of Parliament
as will certainly vote for repealing all the
Tests and Penal Laws touching Religion,
and they hope to steer all their friends
and followers accordingly; so that if the
Lord-Lieutenant will cordially assist with
his influence over the Church party there
cannot be in human reason any doubt of
our electing two such members.

" I nominated to them two such Gentlemen to stand for Burgesses, but (I must
confess) they returned upon me with reiter-
ated desires that I would stand for one,
and therefore rather than the King shall
fail of one to vote for repealing the Tests
and Penal Laws I shall be willing to stand.
The other they desired to stand with me is
Robert Audley, Esq, late Deputy Recorder
of our Town, who when in power was very
indulgent to all Dissenters. I sent yester-

day a letter to him at his howse in Biggles-
ward, but he was gone into Lincolnshire,
and my letter returned. In the next place
we had thoughts of Sir Edmond Gardiner,
our present Recorder, who we humbly
conceive will incline to stand and to vote
for repealing if your Honour be pleased
to send for him, and propose it, especially
if it be made known that it will be no
charge to him that the Lord Lieutenant's
interests shall be conjounct with ours in
the Election. Sir Edmond is now in
London at Lincoln's Inn.

"My zeal against the Tests and Penal
Laws is so fervent that I cannot but
strenuously endeavour in my sphere to
promote the electing of such Members of
Parliament as will certainly damn them,
and therefore what further reasonable instruction I shall receive from your Lord-
shippes to serve my Sovereign in this affair,
shall be with all diligence and faithfulnesse
observed, by, my Lord, Your Honour's
most humble and most faithful servant,

"JOHN ESTON."

"*Bedford.* November 22, 1687." *

* "Life of John Bunyan," Vol. II. pp. 106–8.

It would seem that Bunyan was not unwilling (why should he be?) to accept James's Declaration of Indulgence. But he was not placed in the difficult position of the clergy of the Church of England, who were required to read it from the pulpit. Passive resistance did not fall to his lot this time. He lived peaceably in his habitation in S. Cuthbert's parish, close to where his chapel now stands. Hearne's diary tells of a friend of his, Mr. Bagford, a noted antiquary and, I think, a Nonjuror, whose MSS. were bought after his death by Harley,* visiting Bunyan on purpose to see his study. "When he came John received him very civilly and courteously, but his study consisted only of a Bible and a parcel of books, 'The Pilgrim's Progress' chiefly, written by himself, all lying on a shelf or shelves." During these years he seems to have paid many

* See Ouvry's privately printed "Letters of Hearne," 1874, p. 57.

visits to London. He was a popular
preacher, rivalling by his freedom of expression the more solemn and precise Richard
Baxter. It is of an earlier period presumably that Charles Doe, one of his early
biographers, begins to write when he
says :

" It was at this time of persecution I
heard that Mr. Bunyan came to London
sometimes and preached; and because of
his fame, and I having read some of his
books, I had a mind to hear him. And
accordingly I did at Mr. More's meeting
in a private house; and the text was,
' The fears of the wicked shall come upon
him, but the desires of the righteous shall
be granted.' But I was offended at the
text, because not a New Testament one,
for then I was very jealous of being cheated
by men's sophisticating of Scripture to
serve their turn or opinion, I being then
come into New Testament light in the love
of God and the promises, having had
enough for the present of the historical

and doing for favour in the Old Testament.
But Mr. Bunyan went on, and preached so
New Testament-like that he made me
admire, and weep for joy, and give him
my affections. And he was the first man
that ever I heard preach to my unenlightened
understanding and experience, for methought all his sermons were adapted to
my condition, and had apt similitudes,
being full of the love of God and the manner
of its secret working upon the soul, and of
the soul under the sense of it, that I could
weep for joy most part of his sermons;
and so, by a letter, I introduced myself
into his acquaintance, and, indeed, I have
not since met with a man I have liked so
well. I was acquainted with him but
about three years before he died, and then
missed him sorely."

Apparently Doe means that he heard
him preach some years before he came to
know him. Of the later years he writes :

" When Mr. Bunyan preached in London,
if there were but one day's notice given,

there would be more people come together to hear him preach than the meeting-house could hold. I have seen to hear him preach, by my computation, about twelve hundred at a morning lecture by seven o'clock on a working day, in the dark winter-time. I also computed about three thousand that came to hear him one Lord's Day at London, at a town's-end meeting-house, so that half were fain to go back again for want of room, and then himself was fain at a backdoor to be pulled almost over people to get upstairs to his pulpit."

The description reads like an anticipation of the most popular days of Wesley and Whitefield.

But the busy life was now near its close. In August 1688 he rode to Reading and preached, also doing the good service of reconciling a son, who was a neighbour of his at Bedford, to his father, who had intended to disinherit him. Thence he rode to London, to stay with his friend and co-religionist, John Strudwick, in Snow Hill. On the journey he had been wet through, and seems to have " caught a chill," as laymen, to the annoyance of doctors who cannot supply an explanation, still make bold to say. He preached on August 19. Two days later he fell grievously sick. He bore his sufferings with constancy and patience, and he used the words that Laud had declared on the scaffold to be the most comforting of all texts : " Cupio dissolvi et esse cum Christo." He would say them in English : very likely he would not know that they were the last words of a prelate who trusted as firmly as himself in the Lord Jesus Christ. On Friday, August 31, 1688, he died. And thus the books of his congregation at Bedford make record of their sorrow and observance :

" Wednesday 4th of September was kept in prayre and humilyation for this Heavy Stroak upon us, ye Deathe of deare Brother

Bunyan. Apoynetd also that Wednesday next be kept in praire and humiliation on the same Account."

A week later it added :

" Apoynted that all ye Bretheren meet together on the 18th of this month Septr., to Humble themselves for this Heavy hand of God upon us. And also to pray unto ye Lord for Counsell and Direction what to do in order to seek out for A fitt person to make choyce of for an Elder." " Tuesday ye 18th was the whole congregation mett to Humble themselves before God by ffasting and prayre for his Hevy and Sevear Stroak upon us in takeing away our Honoured Brother Bunyan by death."

Bunyan was buried in the Strudwick vault in Bunhill fields; and the words on his tomb were : " Here lyes the body of Mr. John Bunyan, Author of the ' Pilgrim's Progress,' aged 59, who died Aug. 17, 1688." The date is wrong, and was probably added many years later, when the vault was opened to receive other interments. But Southey gives the epitaph differently and correctly. It is possible he may have seen it before it disappeared.

CERTAINLY Bunyan's life is an interesting one. An unlearned and ignorant man with not a little of the fervour of Christ's Apostles who were so described, he made his way determinedly through the tempests and shoals of life, unyielding, unflinching, never departing an inch from the truth as he saw it, a man of a strong will and a tender heart. Courage undaunted was his, and courage, as so often, won in the end. Such a life of struggle and persistence must be worth study and remembrance. But Bunyan the writer is immortal, Bunyan the man only memorable. The tinker of Elstow might have preached thousands of sermons, or been in prison all his life, and passed into oblivion, if

he had not written one of the great books
in the literature of the world.

"The Pilgrim's Progress" appeared in
its first edition at the end of 1677; within
a year came a new edition with many
additions. In 1684 appeared the Second
Part. Edition followed edition quickly.
Few copies of the earlier ones survive.
They were bought and devoured, one would
think, and handed about till they fell to
pieces. It was long before the world of
literature noticed the book, but among the
people it was a classic from the first.

"The Pilgrim's Progress from this world
to that which is to come delivered under
the similitude of a dream wherein is discovered the manner of his setting out,
his dangerous journey, and safe arrival at
the desired country." How did the main
thought come to Bunyan? It has been
traced, of course, to a medieval origin:
French literature has been ransacked for
examples: similarities in the English writ-

ings of the sixteenth century have been pointed out, and notably in Spenser. It were tedious to recall all that has been said to show that Bunyan was not original. The result is an absurdity. He was most thoroughly original, as Shakespeare and Molière were original. But it may well be that—limited though his reading may have been, and small, as we learn from many sources, his library—he had read, or been told, of the most beautiful expression, in the generation before him, of the great spiritual thought of life as a pilgrimage towards the home of God. That, I think, comes in the " Scala Perfectionis " of the Carthusian Walter Hilton, embodied in the " Sancta Sophia " of Father Baker. This is a passage to be cherished by all who have read it :

" There was a man," saith he, " that had a great desire to go to Jerusalem ; and because he knew not the right way, he addressed himself for advice to one that he hoped was not unskilful in it, and asked him whether there was any way passable thither. The one answered, that the way thither was both long and full of very great difficulties; yea, that there were many ways that seemed and promised to lead thither, but the dangers of them were too great. Nevertheless, one way he knew which, if he would diligently pursue according to the directions and marks that he would give him,—though, said he, I cannot promise thee a security from many frights, beatings, and other ill-usage and temptations of all kinds; but if thou canst have courage and patience enough to suffer them without quarrelling, or resisting, or troubling thyself, and so pass on, having this only in thy mind, and sometimes on thy tongue, *I have nought, I am nought, I desire nought but to be at Jerusalem*—my life for thine, thou wilt escape safe with thy life and in a competent time arrive thither.

" The pilgrim, overjoyed with these news, answered : So I may have my life safe,

and may at last come to the place that I
above all things only desire, I care not
what miseries I suffer in the way. Therefore let me know only what course I am to
take, and, God willing, I will not fail to
observe carefully your directions. The
guide replied : Since thou hast so good a
will, though I myself never was so happy
as to be in Jerusalem, notwithstanding, be
confident that by the instructions that I
shall give thee, if thou wilt follow them,
thou shalt come safe to thy journey's
end." *

So the not unskilful man taught the
pilgrim of old the way to the heavenly
city : and so Evangelist taught Christian.
But with Bunyan the thought is not
expanded into a series of meditations; it
is made the *motif* of a vivacious story.
The quest is spiritual, but all the way is
through material things. It has the human
touch of poetry, such as Raleigh's,

* " Holy Wisdom," by Ven. Father Baker, pp.
58–9.

" Give me a scallop shell of quiet,
      My staff of faith to lean upon,
  My scrip of joy, immortal diet,
      My bottle of salvation,
  My gown of glory, hope's true gage !
      And thus I'll take my pilgrimage."

But certainly the pilgrim-idea is a familiar
one to all Christian ages : we need not
inquire how it came to Bunyan. Certainly, also, Bunyan always had his eyes
and ears open : to see human life and
read books when he could; to hear all men
and women said. For example, it has
often been supposed that he read medieval
romances. Very likely he did not, but he
knew at least of Sir Beves of Hampton.
He took no religious ideas from such a book,
and he did not dabble in dragons or follow
Paynim princesses. Nothing of the plot of
" The Pilgrim's Progress " (if it has a plot)
or of " The Holy War " can be traced to
Sir Beves. But yet there are touches of
romance which show that Bunyan's time
had not all been wasted when he read such
tales.

If he read the romances, he accounted it,
like bell-ringing, as among the sins and
follies of his youth. He makes one of his
own characters—but certainly it is not said
in his condign praise—to call out, " Give
me a ballad, a news book, George on horse-
back, or Bevis of Southampton : give me
some book that teaches curious arts, that
tells old fables."

No literary pedigree certainly can be
traced from Beves, and if Bunyan read it
at all, it must have been in chap-book
form, one of those quaint rough quartos
from which in England, as in Spain, the
people derived all their knowledge of the
medieval romances; and maybe as a ballad.
So Puttenham in " The Art of English
Poesy " (1589) tells of such tales being

" Song to the harpe in places of assembly,
where the company shalbe desirous to
heare of old aduentures and Valiaunces of
noble Knights in times past, as are those of
King *Arthur* and his Knights of the round

table, Sir *Beuys* of *Southampton*, *Guy* of *Warwicke*, and others like."

And again of

. . . " Small & popular musickes song by . . . blind harpers or such like tauerne minstrels that giue a fit of mirth for a groat, & their matters being for the most part stories of old time, as the tale of *Sir Topas*, the reportes of *Beuis* of *Southampton*, *Guy* of *Warwicke*, *Adam Bell*, & *Clymme* of the *Clough*, & such other old Romances or historicall rimes, made purposely for recreation of the common people at Christmasse diners and brideales, & in tauernes & alehouses, & such other places of base resort." *

Certainly Bunyan, though castles and dragons, tempters to infidelity, and bribes to forsake the right way, were constantly in his mind, thought of S. George with no greater reverence than did Gibbon, and,

* Pp. 43 and 87 of Vol. II. of Gregory Smith's " Elizn. Critical Essays " (1904).

with Francis Meres, of Bevis of Hampton
as one of the books " hurtful to youth."

Again, persons not altogether fanciful
have wondered whether Bunyan knew the
beginning of the " Divina Commedia."
" As I walked through the wilderness of
the world," says Bunyan, " I lighted on a
certain place, where was a Den; and I
laid me down in that place to sleep : and
as I slept I dreamed a dream."

> " Tant' era pien di sonno in su quel punto
>   Che la verace via abbandonai,"

says Dante when he entered the " selva
oscura," midway, as Bunyan was, on the
road of life. But there is nothing close
between the two : nothing that you could
not parallel in almost any other two
imaginative writers.

Again, one might inquire what books of
his own time Bunyan had read. There are
quips which remind one of Shakespeare :
nothing, I think, of Milton. The Emblem
writers surely he had met with.

Or, take books much less well known. One wonders whether Bunyan ever saw "Christ's Passion, a Tragedy with Annotations," which was published in 1640. It was written by George Sandys, "Dismist from Arms by an Act of Pim's," and dedicated to King Charles. Sir Sidney Lee's description of it, in the "Dictionary of National Biography," as "a translation in heroic verse from the Latin of Grotius," is not exact. It is by no means throughout either written in heroic verse or a translation from Grotius, whose "steps," Sandys says, "afar off I follow." The great Falkland, his intimate friend, whose companion, Aubrey tells us, he had often been at Great Tew, wrote a poetic eulogy to introduce it, recalling the author's famous travels and his unstained religion—

"Now Thames with Ganges may thy labour praise,
  Which there breed faith and here devotion raise."

Such was Bunyan's aim too, and his laboured verse now and then recalls the stately periods of Sandys : yet though now and then Bunyan may have won a thought from it, " Christ's Passion " is far more akin to " Samson Agonistes " than to anything in the Bedfordshire preacher's poems or theology.

It were idle to continue the quest. Bunyan claims entire originality for himself, and why should we not allow it ? This is his claim, made in " The Holy War " :

" It came from mine own heart, so to my head,
    And thence into my fingers trickled :
    Then to my pen, from whence immediately
On paper I did dribble it daintily.

" Manner and matter too was all mine own ;
    Nor was it unto any mortal known,
    Till I had done it.   Nor did any then
By books, by wits, by tongues, or hand, or pen,
Add five words to it, or wrote half a line
Thereof : the whole and every whit is mine.

" Also for THIS thine eye is now upon,
    The matter in this manner came from none

But the same heart and head, fingers and pen,
As did the other.   Witness all good men,
For none in all the world, without a lie,
Can say that ' this is mine,' excepting I.

" I wrote not this of my ostentation;
Nor cause I seek of men their commendation.
I do it to keep them from such surmise,
As tempt them will my name to scandalize
Witness my name; if anagram'd to thee
The letters make Nu hony in a B.
                              " JOHN BUNYAN."

Turn then to the book itself.   Why is it
a great work of literature?   First, perhaps
because it is written so obviously and
entirely from the heart—" Madam, I swear
I use no art at all."   It seems to tell an
actual experience.   You can believe it all to
have happened, the writer's imagination is so
vivid.   And again, if a man wishes to learn
how to write plainly and directly, to sustain
interest and enforce conviction, where can
he learn better than from the ignorant
tinker?   Abana and Pharpar, to those who
have seen them, are far more lovely than
the Jordan; but Jordan has the saving

grace of life. It is certainly not merely a matter of " style "; yet a matter of style it is. Let us remember what a master in letters has said.

Sir Walter Scott, in his article in the *Quarterly Review*,* says that Southey's eulogy of Bunyan's " homespun style " is a just one. Thus it was :

" Bunyan was confident in his own powers of expression ; he says,

> " thine only way
> Before them all, is to say out thy say
> In thine own native language, which no man
> Now useth, nor with ease dissemble can."

And he might well be confident in it. His is a homespun style, not a manufactured one : and what a difference is there between its homeliness, and the flippant vulgarity of the Roger L'Estrange and Tom Brown school! If it is not a well of English undefiled to which the poet as well as the philologist must repair, if they would drink of the living waters, it is a clear stream of

* Vol. 43, p. 484 ; cf. above, pp. 48–51.

current English,—the vernacular speech of
his age, sometimes indeed in its rusticity
and coarseness, but always in its plainness
and its strength. To this natural style
Bunyan is in some degree beholden for his
general popularity;—his language is every-
where level to the most ignorant reader,
and to the meanest capacity : there is a
homely reality about it; a nursery tale is
not more intelligible, in its manner of
narration, to a child. Another cause of his
popularity is, that he taxes the imagination
as little as the understanding. The vividness of his own, which, as his history shows,
sometimes could not distinguish ideal impressions from actual ones, occasioned this.
He saw the things of which he was writing,
as distinctly with his mind's eye as if they
were indeed passing before him in a dream.
And the reader perhaps sees them more
satisfactorily to himself, because the out-
line of the picture is presented to him, and
the author having made no attempt to fill
up the details, every reader supplies them
according to the measure and scope of his
own intellectual and imaginative powers."

Or, may we not quote the great Johnson, a critic whose every personal opinion must have been poles away from Bunyan's? "This is the great merit of the book," he says, "that the most cultivated man cannot find anything to praise more highly, and the child knows nothing more amusing."

In an interesting revelation of his opinion as to who are the "great unreadables," a famous modern writer has confessed that Jane Austen bores him, that he was glad to have finished "Paradise Lost," and thought "Paradise Regained" unreadable, that he found the perusal of the "Faerie Queene" only to be finished with groans and believes Ruskin to be a crumbling classic. But one rejoices to discover that he places "The Pilgrim's Progress" beside "Robinson Crusoe" and Boswell's "Johnson." Then he gives rather a personal revelation than a reason: "Bunyan's Christian sets off to walk to Heaven alone, which is what every true

Englishman wants to do." Do we—and, be it remembered, all other nations, for "The Pilgrim's Progress" is that one of the three named which is rather an international than an English classic—delight in Bunyan's Pilgrim because he is selfish and wishes only to save his own soul? It may possibly be true that Bunyan entirely lacked any conception of a Church, of hearts linked together in God, of self-sacrifice, of solidarity in religious witness. He was certainly a thorough Protestant, and that may mean a thorough individualist, but quite certainly that is not the reason why his book is so universally beloved.

As these words were being written the present Archbishop of Canterbury was putting forward a much truer ideal for Englishmen—" if from childhood every Christian had been accustomed to think of himself first as a member of a world-wide body, the Christian Church, and of his particular nation as one of so many provinces of the greater whole, nationalism might have been restrained and wars avoided."* Englishmen should be ashamed, and not proud, of wanting to walk off to Heaven alone. The reason for the popularity of "The Pilgrim's Progress" among true Englishmen is because in direct, unaffected yet poetic language it expresses the two most appealing claims upon human interest, reality and romance. Englishmen like to feel that it is those two factors in human life which draw them most. "The Pilgrim's Progress" begins as an allegory : there are those who claim for it (rather absurdly) the position of the first English novel. But it is very soon seen to have beneath the veil of allegory a close and consistent presentation of fact. Christian is no fictitious hero : Christiana and her children are thoroughly human beings : Mr. Great-heart, quite as truly as Mr. Feeble-mind and Mr. Facing-both-ways, walked and

* Reported in *The Times*, Nov. 25, 1927.

M

talked on earth. But all the persons are transfigured by the light of romance : romance always, as Ruskin used the word, in a good sense : romance ennobling fact, as Holman Hunt's babies in the picture of the Innocents are solid, prosaic figures illuminated by a light divine.

The book defies analysis. There is no page that is not significant, hardly a line that is not, for some touch of nature, worth remembering. The dream shows Christian beginning the agony of his soul by reading the Book, urged by Evangelist to fly from the wrath to come, leaving his wife and children, and all that he had, and the neighbours who mocked or threatened. Obstinate rebukes him. Pliable is half persuaded to follow. Indeed he does follow, and listens, and is happy enough with the bright promises made him, till both fall into the Slough of Despond, where, as Bunyan well knew, so many lives have been engulfed. Pliable turned back, but Christian struggled out of the

mire, his face still set towards the wicket-
gate : encouraged by Help, who told him
of the steps and of the sixteen hundred
years in which instructions had been thrown
in to fill up the slough, yet it was as full
as ever of mire and dirt. So knew Mr.
Worldly Wiseman that the slough was but
the beginning of the sorrows that must
beset the pilgrim on his way, which after
all was the wrong way to peace, and
Evangelist a foolish adviser, while Mr.
Legality would far more prudently help
Christian to be rid of the burden on his back.
But as he turned aside to seek this aid, the
hill he was to climb seemed more dangerous
than before, and fires burst from it : and
Evangelist appeared again with stern words
of warning :

> " When Christian unto carnal men gives ear
> Out of their way they go and pay f'r it dear,
> For Master Worldly Wiseman can but show
> A saint the way to bondage and to woe."

He is an alien and Mr. Legality a cheat,
and his son Civility, notwithstanding his

simpering looks, is but a hypocrite and
cannot help.   So Evangelist kissed Pilgrim
farewell, and he came to the wicket-gate,
and he was let through it, and came to
the house of Interpreter, who showed him
the picture of Him who should be his guide.
In the house was a room full of the dust
of sin, which the more it was swept became
the more choking, till the water of the
Gospel was sprinkled upon it.   There also
were the two lads, Passion and Patience :
the one all for the bird in the hand, and
the other one who would have the best
things last.   In the house was the room
where the devil was for ever trying to put
out the fire of grace : and by it the stately
palace where many stately persons walked
and where the valiant man could force his
way :   where too was the professor, the
man of despair, in the iron cage.   Here for
the first time we meet with the bitter
predestinarianism which Bunyan had come
to accept : for the scene ends with the

horrible words of the imprisoned wretch, "God hath denied me repentance: his Word gives me no encouragement to believe: yet himself hath shut me up in this iron cage, nor can all the men in the world let me out. O Eternity, Eternity! how shall I grapple with the misery that I must meet with in Eternity?" Then one more vision for the Interpreter: a picture of the dread last day. And lo! Christian rids himself and betakes him again to his journey. Onward: and the very sight of the Cross lifts his burden from him: and three shining ones tell him that his sins are forgiven, give him a change of raiment and a sealed roll which shall pass him through the celestial gate. But on the way he sees Simple, Sloth and Presumption asleep, with fetters on their heels, who had each a word for him which showed that they too were outside salvation: I see no danger: a little more sleep: and Every Fat must stand upon

his own bottom. Then over a wall tumbled
Formality and Hypocrisy, who found the
way that he had taken too far round for
them, and the coat he wore needless;
because Laws and Ordinances would ensure
them admission to the King's house. When
they came to the foot of the hill they would
not take the steep way, but one that of
Danger, the other that of Destruction, and
so miserably perished. Timorous and Mis-
trust too turned back as Christian came to
the rest-house where he was to find his
first repose.

What a delightful description is that of
the House Beautiful. Bunyan, one fancies,
had little care for æsthetics, yet here for
once his eyes were opened to things which
many men enjoy. Beyond the Hill Difficulty was a pleasant arbour made by the
Lord of the Hill for the refreshing of weary
travellers: like those banquet-houses the
seventeenth century was so fond of, as at
Chipping Camden, whence the dwellers

took their ease and looked out upon trim
garden plots. There Christian slept. But
when he was up again to draw nigh to the
house there were two lions in the way.
The approach to Beauty is fringed with
perils. And—for he slept in the daytime—
Christian had lost his Roll, without which
he could not win entrance to the House.
A very stately palace it was, and when he
was come within sight of the porter's
lodge, lo! the lions were chained. Damsels, as beautiful and as decorous as those
in "Gryll Grange," received him. The
first of them was Discretion, and with her
and Prudence and the rest he had happy
talk and no small refreshment at a table
furnished with fat things and with wine
well refined. Next morning were to be
seen the Rareties of the place—chiefly the
fine library, and the records in the study,—
the armour and the "furniture" for the
pilgrims, and, a day later, the view of the
Delectable Mountains, with the woods and

vineyards, the flowers and fruit of Immanuel's Land, and our little country birds
are heard—at springtime, when the flowers
appear and the sun shines warm.

Houghton Park has a house, now in ruins,
which in modern times seems to have been
regarded as the "true originall" of the
House Beautiful. It is not impossible.
The other day *The Times* described it and
its history well. Thus :

"Houghton House was originally designed in 1615 for the Countess of Pem-
broke, 'Sidney's sister,' by John Thorpe,
working between 1570 and 1632, whose
best known works in a long list are Holland
House, Kensington, and Audley End, Essex.
For some reason Thorpe did not complete
Houghton House, and there is little doubt
that the two stone loggias, of which considerable portions remain, were added by
Inigo Jones with other improvements to
the brick structure as left by Thorpe.
Precise documentary evidence is wanting
in both cases, but it is known that Thorpe

was engaged in building Toddington Manor
and had prepared plans for remodelling
Ampthill Castle early in the seventeenth
century, and the plan and character of
Houghton House correspond with his manner; while the style of Inigo Jones is not
less manifest in the additions, the centre
of the north front being similar to the
interior of the Convent della Carita at
Venice, by Palladio. Thus, like Castle
Ashby, Northants, reputed to be by Thorpe,
to which Inigo Jones added a fourth side in
1624, Houghton House, even in its present
condition, illustrates that sudden leap from
Jacobean to Anglo-Classic which was one
of the most striking developments in our
architecture, and as an example of the
earlier manner of the architect of the Ban-
queting House, Whitehall, it is of excep-
tional interest to students.

"From 1630 to 1674 Houghton House
was occupied by the Bruce family, being
sold to the Earl of Aylesbury in 1675 and
to the Duke of Bedford in 1738. In 1765
Sir William Chambers, the architect of
Somerset House, was called in by the

Marquess of Tavistock to repair the house and alter the interior apartments in the west wing, and for some years after the death of the Marquess in the hunting field it was the residence of Lord Ossory. In 1794 Francis, the fifth Duke of Bedford, decided to dismantle the house, the roof being torn off and the great staircase removed to the Swan Inn at Bedford, and from that time the remains have been exposed to weather and vandalism, though a goodly portion of the fabric still exists."

It is interesting that the lady who lived there when Bunyan was young and had just returned home from the Army was named Christiana. She was Countess of Devonshire. It is pleasant to associate this beautiful fragment, and its history, with the house of Bunyan's dream, wherein were all things lovely and of good report. There seems fair hope that what remains of it will be preserved.

But back again to the Pilgrim. In the house he fought his battles over again, as

travellers will; and the wise damsels questioned with him, and corrected him, as
wise damsels do all the world over, and
Christian is brought to something like confession of a selfishness in the beginning of
his flight. Had he done all he could for
his wife and children? What says he?

The didactic damsels must needs, as
their theology demanded, excuse him. And
so they sat talking till supper-time— a scene
somewhat suggestive, perhaps, of the
sumptuous refreshments, a century and
more later, of the good folk of Clapham.

"Indeed I cannot commend my life;
for I am conscious to myself of many fail-
ings: therein, I know also that a man by
his conversation may soon overthrow what
by argument or perswasion he doth labour
to fasten upon others for their good: Yet,
this I can say, I was very wary of giving
them occasion, by any unseemly action, to
make them averse to going on a Pilgrimage.
Yea, for this very thing, they would tell
me I was too precise, and that I denied

myself of sins (for their sakes) in which
they saw no evil. Nay, I think I may say,
that, if what they saw in me did hinder
them, it was my great tenderness in sinning
against God, or of doing any wrong to my
Neighbour."

" Christian's good conversation before
his Wife and Children," says the margin.

The vividness of the tale increases every
step as it goes on. The Valley of Humiliation, which is the test of all loyal hearts,
leads to the Valley of the Shadow of
Death, which none can avoid. Courage :
the thought of Christian is the poet's

> " I sing to think this is the way
>   Unto my Saviour's face."

But before that he must meet Apollyon—
this seems to have been suggested through
one of the romances ; and certainly in
none of them was there so fine a dragon-
like creature, so fierce and hideous, so dis-
dainful and argumentative too.   Christian
comes from his land, the City of Destruction:

cujus regio ejus religio, said the men of
Bunyan's time, Protestants as well as
Catholics, Richelieu and the Lion of the
North. But Christian would none of that :
" I have let myself unto another, even the
King of Princes." So they must needs
fight, and " in this combat no man can
imagine, unless he has seen and heard, as
I did, what yelling and hideous roaring
Apollyon made all the time of the fight."
Christian is sore wounded, yet must needs
overthrow the wicked one : " but it was
the most dreadful fight that ever I saw."
What an opportunity it gives to the illus-
trators, and what a delight to the lads
who read ! Bunyan had not been a soldier,
any more than he had been a doubter, for
nothing. All his experience goes hotfoot
into his book. Nothing is more beautiful,
more real, in the whole book than those
moments in the hard Valley of Humiliation
and in the darkness over which death always
spreads his wings. Yet they are passed

through; the first danger is over; and beyond it lie the blood, bones, ashes and mangled bodies of the pilgrims that had been slain by Pope and Pagan, the one now dead, the other old and crazy in his joints and biting his nails because he could not come at the pilgrims as they went by. The wish, with Bunyan, was father to the thought. The Popes of Bunyan's day may not all have been very good men, but there was a new life in the Catholic Church overseas which by the way of saintliness should lead many souls to God. Yet perhaps the Englishman's grim humour was not very far wrong when he heard the old man who sat at the mouth of the cave say to him, " You will never mend till more of you be burnt." A Roman Catholic writer, Father Ronald Knox, has recently reasserted that his Church will not waive all right of "invoking the secular arm" or the right to " deport or imprison."

Christian caught up his honoured and

well-beloved brother Faithful, and they
sped on the way together, talking of the
old home and those, good and bad, whom
they had left behind. Faithful has been
beset by the lusts of the flesh, very deadly
and alluring, from which he was saved only
by One who came by, with the holes in his
hands and in his side : " Then I concluded
that he was our Lord." Faithful, indeed,
on his way had learned many things : best
of all, perhaps, that " Shame tells me what
men are, but it tells me nothing what God,
or the word of God, is." Then comes a
picture, Dutch in its realism, of Mr.
Talkative, the son of Mr. Saywell, who
dwelt in Prating Row. " *Ibam via sacra* " :
it was not the first time that a traveller
therein met with such an one. Talkative
will talk theology most impressively; not
only that, but " things heavenly, or things
earthly; things moral, or things evangelical;
things sacred, or things profane; things
past, or things to come; things foreign, or

things at home; things more essential, or
things circumstantial; provided that all be
done to our profit." In good sooth, "It is
better to deal with a Turk than with him."
Bunyan never forgets that good works are
a necessity. He sees in Talkative a bear
that cheweth the cud, but "as the hare, he
retaineth the foot of the dog or bear, and
therefore he is unclean." A very long
conversation it is; but it is not a tedious
one, because it shows the writer in his
acutest and most observant humour. Faithful is parted from at last by Talkative as
"some peevish or melancholy man not fit
to be discoursed with." Evangelist, the
preacher, replaces the babbler, and shows
the difference between wise counsel and
mere cackling. When Christian and Faithful leave the Wilderness they come to
Vanity Fair, a most vivacious picture of the
scenes that Dickens loved and of a town as it
was in later Stewart days. The whole
town was moved at the sight of them, for,

as with the Puritans in Ben Jonson, a fair
was the very thing against which they must
needs protest. Whereat they were hustled
and badgered, and beaten and hung with
chains, and haled before the Judge, Lord
Hategood, who heard the evidence of Envy
and Superstition and Pickthank, just as
Bunyan may have thought his own judges
had heard before. Treason against the noble
Lord Beelzebub and his honourable friends,
all Lords, Old Man, Carnal Delight, Luxur-
ious, Desire of Vain Glory, the old Lord
Lechery and Sir Having Greedy—not so
unlike a picture of the Court of Charles II.
Now the jury, being of wicked men, was hot
against the Pilgrims; and Bunyan enjoys
himself again with the names.

"Then went the Jury out, whose names
were, Mr. Blind-man, Mr. No-good, Mr.
Malice, Mr. Love-lust, Mr. Live-loose, Mr.
Heady, Mr. High-mind, Mr. Enmity, Mr.
Lyar, Mr. Cruelty, Mr. Hate-light, and Mr.
Implacable, who everyone gave in his private

N

Verdict against him among themselves, and afterwards unanimously concluded to bring him in guilty before the Judge. And first Mr. Blind-man the Foreman said, I see clearly that this man is an Heretick. Then said Mr. No-good, Away with such a fellow from the Earth. Ay, said Mr. Malice, for I hate the very looks of him. Then said Mr. Love-lust, I could never endure him, Nor I, said Mr. Live-loose, for he would always be condemning my way. Hang him, hang him, said Mr. Heady. A sorry Scrub, said Mr. High-mind. My heart riseth against him, said Mr. Enmity. He is a Rogue, said Mr. Lyar. Hanging is too good for him, said Mr. Cruelty. Let's despatch him out of the way, said Mr. Hate-light. Then said Mr. Implacable, Might I have all the world given me, I could not be reconciled to him, therefore let us forthwith bring him in guilty of death; And so they did, therefore he was presently condemned, To be had from the place where he was, to the place from whence he came, and there to be put to the most cruel death that could be invented."

And so, through these wicked men, the worst things on earth befell Faithful: torture and death. But then the hereafter that belongs to a martyr's end :

" Now, I saw that there stood behind the multitude a Chariot and a couple of Horses, waiting for Faithful, who (so soon as his adversaries had dispatched him) was taken up into it, and straightway was carried up through the Clouds, with sound of Trumpet, the nearest way to the Celestial Gate."

And Christian, who somehow escaped, must then go on alone, yet not for long, for one Hopeful, who had seen the witness that he bore, joined him on the way ; and their first adventure is the meeting with the intelligent Mr. By-ends, an enduring character in the experience of us all, who will never go against wind and tide, but has the luck to " jump with the present way of the times," and has for companion Mr. Hold-the-way, Mr. Money-love, Mr. Save-all, each a former

schoolfellow of his under Mr. Gripe-man.
And they discuss together how one may
serve God and Mammon; but Christian
gives them a straight, unyielding answer;
and very sharply indeed, too, does he speak
to their friend Mr. Demon, who dwells by
a silver mine; but Christian will have none
of the silver, for he remembers Lot's wife
and indeed sees the very pillar that was
made of her. So on by a river, one of
Bunyan's most beautiful descriptions, to
By-path Meadow, where they foolishly
turn aside, led by Vain-confidence, who
perished for his error. Back again to the
highway, and in the morning Mr. Doubting
Castle, beset by Giant Despair, who, by
the advice of his wicked wife, beat them
sorely till Christian, counselled by the
Giant, even thought of suicide; but Hopeful helped him again to pluck up the heart
of a man. The Key of Promise unlocked the
prison door, and they set off again towards
the Delectable Mountain, in Immanuel's

Land, and within sight of his City. Led
by the Shepherds, Knowledge, Experience,
Watchful and Sincere, they passed safely
by the Hill called Error, where many had
been dashed to pieces, and the byway to
hell. Those whom they met now were often
going to the Celestial City, but by some
deceiving path, so that they never reached
it, such as that very brisk country lad
Ignorance and others who refused all
guidance; whereas Christian (perhaps a
little tediously) instructed the worthy
Hopeful as to other men's sins, and they took
a wrong turning, and were snared in the
Flatterer's net, till a Shining One released
them after a sound chastisement. Still
there are pitfalls in Christian's way, even
though he draws nigh to the heavens; and
Atheist " falls into very great laughter that
they think there is any such place at all,
but they turned away from him," and he,
laughing at them, went his way. Ignorance
was still following them, and they turned

from their own talk of help and comfort to instruct him. He proves a very skilful inquirer, ready with answers which have not a little truth in them, in reliance on faith and love of God; but Bunyan's Calvinism will not allow Christian to give the poor lad any hope, and they pass on, till they have a perfect view of the City, which makes them sick with very love.

Yet still there is the deep river to cross, with no bridge, and the deep waters fill Christian with fears and temptations of despair. Hopeful cheers him, and the two Shining Ones meet them as they come forth and lead them up the hill, talking of the glory of that place where the beauty and glory were inexpressible. So to the gate, with the King's trumpeters around them, compassing them about with ten thousand welcomes. All is glory and beauty; yet still it is with a sad heart that we find poor Ignorance, who had come along without any encouragement, seized by the Shining

Ones and carried through the air to a door in the hill. " Then I saw that there was a way to Hell, even from the gates of Heaven, as well as from the City of Destruction." Bunyan never feared to see whole the dangers and the tragedy of life. " So I awoke, and behold it was a dream."

Here ends the first " Pilgrim's Progress," the triumph of the genius of the Bedfordshire " brasyer." Bunyan must have felt how great a thing he had done; everything he says of it shows how he loved his work. Its first form, " printed for Nath. Ponder at the Peacock in the Poultry, near Cornhil, 1678," of which only two copies are known to exist,* was soon added to; and the additions are among the best parts of the book as we know it now.

It was in the same year, 1678, that the First Part of " The Pilgrim's Progress " was printed in two editions. The second con-

* It probably appeared at the end of 1677, old style, in February. There is a facsimile reprint (Eliot Stock, no date).

tains all of Mr. Worldly Wisdom and Mr.
Diffidence, much more of Mr. By-ends, more
of the good talk of Charity with Christian,
and of Evangelist, the name of the Hill
Difficulty, the pillar of Lot's wife, and the
outburst of the bells and the trumpets at
the coming to the Celestial City. These are
all improvements. And the subject, one
may be sure, was never out of the writer's
mind.

The Second Part did not come out till
six years after. It tells " The manner of
the setting out of Christian's Wife and
Children, their dangerous journey and safe
arrival at the desired country." Froude
thought it " but a feeble reverberation of the
first." That is a harsh judgment. More
sentimental it doubtless is, but it is a relief
to have less unbroken sternness; and the
characters, the delightful children, whom we
watch as they grow up on their journey,
the love-makings, and the humanity of it
all, should make it no less lovable a book
than its forerunner. There are even more

touches of nature in it. The dream begins
with a walk with an old man through the
woods, who tells what men have heard
of Christian's adventure and happiness.
Christiana too dreamed, and of two ill-
favoured ones who stood beside her bed,
fearing to lose her as they had lost her
husband. Needless to tell the variations
of the journey on which she now led her
children. Through them all Bunyan shows
as much skill in humorous portraiture as
before: Mrs. Timorous, Mrs. Bat's eyes,
Mrs. Inconsiderate, Mrs. Light-mind, and
Mrs. Know-nothing, and worse women than
that.

Christiana, our heroine, is the contrast
to these; and it has been suggested that
in her Bunyan drew a loving picture of his
second wife, while in Mercy, her companion,
he remembered Mary, the wife of his youth.

Thus he writes of women:
" I will say again, that when the Saviour
was come women rejoyced in him before
either man or angel. I read not that even

any man did give unto Christ so much as one groat, but the women followed him and ministered to him of their substance. 'Twas a woman that washed his feet with tears, and a woman that anointed his body to the burial. They were women that wept when he was going to the Cross; and women that followed him from the Cross and that sat by his sepulchre when he was buried. They were women that was first with him at his Resurrection morn, and women that brought tidings first to his disciples that he was risen from the dead. Women, therefore, are highly favoured, and show by these things that they are sharers with us in the grace of life.''

With such thoughts it was that Bunyan sent his Second Part into the world, to learn from Christiana and from Mercy too, for of her he wrote :

" Yea, let young damsels learn of her to prize
      The world which is to come, in any wise.
    When little tripping maidens follow God,
    And leave old doting sinners to his rod,
    It is like those old days when the young outcried,
    Hosanna ! to whom old ones did deride.''

Derived it may be from his brave wife, Elizabeth, there is certainly a more gracious spirit in this Second Part than in the First; and that most of all in the constant mention of children, the loving knowledge of their ways, and the eyes more open to the beauties of earth and sky.

Mercy talks sweetly in the summer parlour to which the Keeper of the Gate admits them all: and there is speech of the timid maid and the open-eyed children on the savage dog which the wicked neighbour keeps to awe pilgrims, if so it be, out of the right way. Apples interest children quite as much as dogs, and ere long they suffer as much from fruit as from quadrupeds. At the Interpreter's House there is again a warm welcome, with many an acted parable—the spider with her venom, the chickens with their thankful upward look, the sheep with her lesson of unmurmuring patience: the lessons, too, of the garden and the field, of the robin with the spider, of the tree that is rotten in heart. So to supper,

with the minstrel singing at the meal.
Supper ended, it was time for bed. The
women lay singly alone, the boys by themselves, and Mercy could not sleep for joy.
And the next morning, a good bath in the
garden, in one of those lovely stone imita-
tions of classical times which delighted the
seventeenth century—as among the shades
of Packwood in Warwickshire, where the
Dugdales lived in Bunyan's day. When
they went on their way the Interpreter
sent with them Greatheart, the finest
character in the book, a soldier to the
finger-tips, delighting, as his creator must
have done, in the trappings as well as in
the feats of war. The rest of the story is
really the record of this hero, ready to
teach the theology of Christ, rightly dividing
the word of truth, as well as using the sword
of the Spirit and wearing the whole armour
of God. There is, no doubt, a constant and
rather confusing mixture of allegory and fact,
of the very Christ as pictured in the Gospels,

and the imagery which the writer employs
to illustrate his work. It is needless to
dwell on this. Bunyan's theology, if sometimes fierce and narrow, is always genuine
and a real endeavour to justify God's ways
to man. The one aspect is seen in the
hanging of Simple, Sloth and Presumption ;
the other in the renewed charm and peace-
fulness of the House Beautiful. Pure
romance begins again : the lions who
frighten the boys ; Giant Grim ; more eating,
of lamb, raisins and figs ; and drinking, of
spirits and wine ; Mercy's instructive
dream ; Prudence's catechising the children,
with touches in it that suggest the Shorter
Catechism ; Mercy's unsatisfactory sweet-
heart, Mr. Brisk, " a man of some breeding,
that pretended to religion, but a man that
stuck very close to the world " : Skill, the
physician who was called in to correct the
excesses of little Matthew with his Universal
Pill ; and then the boys turning the tables
on Prudence and asking her many questions,

to which she gave discreet answers. Romance, allegory, human nature, dogma, are intertwined subtilly. The rest of the way is as of old, the Valley of Humiliation, the valley beautiful in lilies, and now a monument where Christian overthrew Apollyon; still all the terrors—and worse—of the passage, with the brave boy Samuel speaking like a man ; the Giant Maul, most terrible of his race; good Father Honest, kind, as the Interpreter had been who stroked their faces, to the boys; poor Mr. Fearing, who was dumpish at the House Beautiful, Gaius at the Guest house, and many more. Startled we may be at first to find Master Matthew old enough to marry Mercy, but there is no measuring time in dreams. What Bunyan measures is bravery and loyalty and truth. More giants to be slain; that well-meaning fellow Feeble-mind to be succoured ; more meals, and more meadows by the riverside ; a tale that never lacks variety, and goes on always with an

inexpressible *joie de vivre*, for so there must
be now that Doubting Castle is destroyed.
Yet still more fighting and a new hero
in Valiant, for, Truth; the song, almost
Shakespearian in its melody, a delightful
simple thing that every child can take
pleasure in :

> " Who would true valour see
>   Let him come thither ;
> One here will constant be ;
>   Come wind, come weather
>   Follow the Master.
> There's no discouragement
> Shall make him once relent
> His first avowed intent
>   To be a pilgrim.
>
> " Who so beset him round
> With dismal stories,
> Do but themselves confound—
>   His strength the more is.
> No lion can him fright,
> He'll with a giant fight,
> But he will have a right
>   To be a pilgrim.
>
> " Hobgoblin nor foul fiend
> Can daunt his spirit,
> He knows, he at the end
>   Shall life inherit.

Then fancies flee away,
He'll fear not what men say,
He'll labour night and day
    To be a pilgrim." *

Thus cheered, the pilgrims go on to the Enchanted Ground.

New experience they had of arbours to tempt as well as to refresh. There was "the Slothful's Friend." Avoid it! And their good guide led them past it, with his map of all the ways and his tinder-box in hand to light him. On to another arbour where idle pilgrims were asleep and would not heed; "and for aught I know they will lie till they rot." Another danger, Madam Bubble in very pleasant attire, though old, who loves banquets, has her hand ever in her pocket fingering her money; many hath she brought to the halter and ten thousand times more to hell. Standfast is with them now, whose coming we hardly

* It is rather amusing to see how the moderns have not only taken away the Shakespearean touch, but spoilt the simplicity of the rest in their attempt to make what they take to be a hymn of it.

noticed, when they found him at prayer, and Greatheart bid join them.

At last the Land of Beulah, all the King's own, all full of freedom and happiness, with all beautiful things, from Camphire with Spikenard that the Magdalen bought, Calamus that Whitman was to make the emblem of pure friendship, and the rest, perfuming their rooms. So to the riverside, and Christiana must say farewell to her children and her friends, the road full of chariots and horses, to see her take her journey, and so she entered the river with a beckon of farewell. One by one the pilgrims followed her, the weak no less bravely than the strong : Mr. Reason-to-halt, Mr. Feeblemind, Mr. Despondency, Mr. Honest, Mr. Valiant and Mr. Standfast. Of these last there are words which have become the most famous in our memories of heroic death. "As he went down deeper he said, 'Grave, where is thy victory?' So he passed over and all the trumpets sounded for him on

o

the other side." A few more lines, tame
in comparison, and Pilgrim's tale is done.

Up and down the story there is abundance
of things not to be forgotten : the man
with the muck rake : Christiana playing
upon the viol and Mercy upon the lute :
Ready-to-halt and Much-afraid taught to
dance upon their way : Fool and Want-
wit washing an Ethiopian " with intention
to make him white, but the more they
washed the blacker he was;" perhaps best
of all, the fresh and well-favoured shepherd's
boy who sang, as Mr. Greatheart made them
listen :

> " He that is down needs fear no fall,
>   He that is low, no pride ;
> He that is humble ever shall
>   Have God to be his guide.
>
> I am content with what I have,
>   Little be it or much ;
> And, Lord, contentment shall I crave,
>   Because thou gavest such.
>
> Fulness to such a burden is
>   That go on Pilgrimage,
> Here little, and hereafter bliss
>   Is best from age to age."

" Do you hear him ? I will dare to say, this boy lives a merrier life, and wears more of that herb called *Heartsease* at his bosom than he that is clad in silk and velvet."

Such a summary as this shows nothing of the extraordinary faithfulness and felicity of the picture of the sturdy soul struggling through toil and temptation towards the right. The Pilgrim is like Everyman of the older generation. He shows what life is, how men go through it, how they draw on to death and the beyond. But as Everyman is the Catholic, the Pilgrim is the Protestant. If there is much that the Pilgrim loses, there is not a little that he fulfils. It is not quite unworthy, different in its whole and texture though it is, to stand beside " The Imitation of Christ."

Each was the work of a man quite obscure when he wrote it. It is curious how little was known of Bunyan in his own day, not only in his drab and dirty youth, but in his

latter years of preaching and authorship.
Crowds came then to hear him preach, and
no doubt, as the many editions prove,
hundreds read " The Pilgrim's Progress."
As to the popularity of his other writings it
is not easy to guess. Professor Masson had
read widely in seventeenth-century books,
and this is what he says :

" John Bunyan : aetat 33 :—Here and
there, up and down the country, people
had heard of a vehement Baptist preacher
of this name, who had been a tinker,
a Parliamentarian soldier, and one knew
not what else. Here and there too
some pious Christians may have been
deriving edification from such specimens
of the tinker's marrowy theology as were
in print, e.g. his ' Few Sights from Hell,'
or the ' Groans of a Damned Soul,' published in Sept. 1658, and his ' Doctrine of
the Law and Grace ' published in May 1659.
It was in Bedford jail, however, where they
were to keep him, more or less closely, a
prisoner from November 1660 to March

1672, that Bunyan was to begin his immortal dreamings." *

Certainly no sign of popularity then. Hardly had it begun ten years later, at least in any extended ways.

Yet he himself foresaw it. He wrote, at the beginning of the Second Part, about his Pilgrim, who seemed to him a living man :—

" City and country will him entertain
  With, Welcome, Pilgrim; yea, they can't refrain
  From smiling, if my Pilgrim be but by,
  Or shows his head in any company.
  Brave gallants do my Pilgrim hug and love,
  Esteem it much, yea, value it above
  Things of a greater bulk; yea, with delight,
  Say, My lark's leg is better than a kite.

" Young ladies, and young gentlewomen too,
  Do no small kindness to my Pilgrim show.
  Their cabinets, their bosoms and their hearts,
  My Pilgrim has, 'cause he to them imparts
  His pretty riddles in such wholesome strains,
  As yields them profit double to their pains
  Of reading; yea, I think I may be bold
  To say, some prize him far above their gold.

" The very children that do walk the street,
  If they do but my holy Pilgrim meet,

* Masson, " Life of Milton," Vol. VI. p. 315.

Salute him will, will wish him well, and say,
He is the holy stripling of the day.

" They that have never seen him, yet admire
What they have heard of him, and much desire
To have his company, and hear him tell
Those pilgrim stories which he knows so well.

" Yea, some who did not love him at the first,
But call'd him fool and noddy, say they must,
Now they have seen and heard him, him commend.
And to those whom they love they do him send.

" Wherefore, my Second Part, thou need'st not be
Afraid to show thy head; none can hurt thee,
That wish but well to him that went before,
'Cause thou com'st after with a second store
Of things as good, as rich, as profitable
For young, for old, for stagg'ring, and for stable."

Bunyan, no doubt, was laughed at in his own day. What is more absurd, thought the Cavalier, than a tinker who leaves his pots and pans to write tales of fancy : quite as absurd as when

" The oyster women locked their fish up
And trudg'd away to cry ' no bishop.' "

Indeed the writer of " The Pilgrim's Progress " had actually served under Hudibras himself, for that ridiculous knight was

no other than Sir Samuel Luke, who commanded at Newport Pagnell. Butler had
been tutor in his household, and it is quite
possible may have seen Bunyan and mocked
at him among the motley ragged crew that
he has branded with his derision. But
Magnano, a magician as well as a tinker, is
not recognisable as Bunyan, and the jests
at the sectaries, particularly the Presbyterians and Independents, are too general to
wring the Pilgrim's withers. It is likely
enough, though Bunyan might have said,

> " What makes a ' Church a den of thieves ' ?
>   A dean and chapter and white sleeves.
>   And what would serve, if those were gone
>   To make it orthodox ?   Our own,"

that Butler had never so much as heard of
" The Pilgrim's Progress."

For the " immortal dreamings " seem to
have taken long to become known. " The
Pilgrim's Progress " was published in 1677,
and two more editions appeared within two
years ; but probably they were little read

at first by educated men and women, whose taste in literature is often decidedly prim. The library of Laud's College at Oxford is rich in seventeenth-century literature, for the Archbishop was a voracious book lover, and a generous benefactor. Of course he did not live to hear of Bunyan, but his interest in books was kept up by his successors. Yet even to-day the library contains only one copy of the famous book, and that is a translation into Hebrew. Not a single copy of any of his other works is there.

There is no reference at all to Bunyan in the multitudinous memoranda of Pepys, nor does Evelyn seem ever to have heard of him.

Another famous seventeenth-century library is that collected by Bishop Morley of Winchester, who died in 1684 and bequeathed his books to his cathedral church. There is no copy of any of Bunyan's works in it. Bunyan's immense popularity with later generations was not of early growth.

Still more remarkable, perhaps, is the

fact that even among the eminent persons
who did not conform to the Church of
England he was certainly not well known.
Mr. F. J. Powicke in his very full life of
Richard Baxter says :

" So far as I know, Baxter nowhere
mentions Bunyan nor Bunyan Baxter.
Yet they were the two greatest spirits in
Puritanism, its two most famous preachers,
its two most influential writers. By 1672
' The Saints' Rest ' had come to its eleventh
edition and the ' Call to the Unconverted '
its thirteenth edition ; while at least
Bunyan's ' Grace Abounding to the Chief
of Sinners,' published in 1666, had spread
far and wide. But Baxter does not refer
to it, nor has he a word to say about ' The
Pilgrim's Progress,' subsequent to its
appearance in 1678. Bunyan, too, is
equally silent about anything written by
Baxter. True, they did not openly assail
each other, and this may be taken to imply
a degree of mutual respect ; but had they
not resolved, by a sort of tacit consent, to
ignore each other ? Moreover, after 1672,
when Bunyan was released from Bedford

Gaol, and Baxter removed from Totteridge
to Bloomsbury, they might easily have met."

But apparently they never did. Bunyan,
year after year, when he came to London,
was extraordinarily popular. Mr. Powicke
speaks of a " Bunyan-furore." Baxter never
mentions him. Mr. Powicke thinks this
was the *odium theologicum*. Is it possible
that it was something like jealousy? Bunyan
had attacked Baxter's friend Fowler, then
at S. Giles's, Cripplegate, afterwards Bishop
of Gloucester, and Baxter resented Bunyan's attack on him, which had ended in a
pamphlet retort entitled " Dirt Wiped Off:
Or a manifest discovery of the gross
ignorance, erroneous and most un-Christian
spirit of one John Bunyan, Lay Reader in
Bedford." Baxter held aloof from Bunyan
" when he saw him, with the air of a Pope,
pouring out his vials of wrath on a man
whom he esteemed both for his own sake
and for his teaching." It is strange, indeed,
that two religious men whose whole interest

in life was theological, and each of whom according to his lights gave himself up to the conversion of souls, should have been so far apart.

Again, it is strange that, sharp though Bunyan's controversy with the Quaker was, George Fox should never once have mentioned him in his Diary. Indeed, so long as he lived, the most popular of all English seventeenth-century writers seems to have remained John the obscure.

In fact Bunyan's fame came late, but it has endured. It began low down and it has risen. As Macaulay puts it—

" The fame of Bunyan during his life, and during the century which followed his death, was indeed great, but was almost entirely confined to religious families of the middle and lower classes. Very seldom was he during that time mentioned with respect by any writer of great literary eminence. Young coupled his prose with the poetry of the wretched D'Urfey. In the ' Spiritual Quixote,' the adventures of

Christian are ranked with those of Jack the
Giant-Killer and John Hickathrift. Cow-
per ventured to praise the great allegorist,
but did not venture to name him.   It is a
significant circumstance that, till a recent
period, all the numerous editions of ' The
Pilgrim's Progress ' were evidently meant
for the cottage and the servants' hall.   The
paper, the printing, the plates, were all
of the meanest description. In general,
when the educated minority and the common people differ about the merit of a book,
the opinion of the educated minority finally
prevails.   ' The Pilgrim's Progress ' is perhaps the only book about which, after the
lapse of a hundred years, the educated
minority has come over to the opinion of
the common people."

And " the common people " has not only
taught (as it often does) its supposed
superiors, but spread its knowledge over the
world.   In these mean editions it spread :
printed in every out of the way place—
I have one produced by the Mozleys at

Gainsborough in 1818, with the spurious Third Part and not a few impudent alterations. What did that matter? Even John Wesley must " improve " it.

Since then " The Pilgrim's Progress " has been translated into a hundred and eighteen languages. The Religious Tract Society has spread it widely over the world. They quote a story from a missionary of Uganda, which runs thus :

" One day, during one of those long itinerating tours, we had to pass along a terrible road which passed over miles of swamp. The only way to traverse these swamps is to be carried on the shoulders of native bearers, with your feet well out. After some time in this most uncomfortable position, with my back nearly breaking, I told my bearers to put me down as I could not hold on any longer. Happily there was a tree trunk close handy, and they deposited me safely upon this, and I was able to rest for a time. Mr. Fisher, however, was less fortunate; he was being carried on the shoulders of his bearers, when one slipped, with the result that my husband took a header into the mud. One of the natives who had been carrying me turned round and said, ' Oh, mistress, poor " Bani " is like Christian in the Slough of Despond.' I only give you these instances to show how the people are assimilating the teaching of the ' Pilgrim's Progress.' The volume is their faithful friend."

And they, very happily as I think, add, after telling many quaintnesses which occur in the translation and illustrations of the book :

" There are thousands of folk in obscure corners of the earth who will never meet an Englishman in this life, but in the next there will be one Englishman whom they will all greet as an old friend and companion —John Bunyan, the tinker of Bedford."

True, one hopes, of the Jesuits as well as the Wesleyans, of all church folk and all sects. For all have tried to make " The Pilgrim's Progress " their own.

Macaulay laughs at Tractarians and Jesuits for botching " The Pilgrim's Progress " with their own ideas. It is quite true that " The Pilgrim's Progress " gives a very inadequate view of theology as taught by the Catholic Church. So the attempt to supplement it, if it is to be used for spiritual edification and instruction, is natural and even necessary. But a better way to regard the book is to get away from the method of the young man who preaches his first sermon and tries to compress into it a whole Body of Divinity and a whole Duty of Man. Take " The Pilgrim's Progress " as it stands, and do not try to extract from it what is not there, or to pretend it is there, or to farce it with spices even the best. Take this, as all other books, for what it is, not for what it is not. Correct it only, as your knowledge enables you to do, when it is obviously wrong or incomplete.

May one not end, as one turns away from "The Pilgrim's Progress," with Bunyan's own words :

" Wouldst thou divert thyself from melancholy?
 Wouldst thou be pleasant, yet be far from folly?
 Wouldst thou read riddles and their explanation?
 Or else be drowned in thy contemplation?
 Dost thou love picking meat?   Or wouldst thou see
 A man i' the clouds, and hear him speak to thee?
 Wouldst thou be in a dream, and yet not to sleep?
 Or wouldst thou in a moment laugh and weep?
 Wouldst thou lose thyself and catch no harm,
 And find thyself again without a charm?
 Wouldst read thyself, and read thou know'st not
     what?
 And yet know whether thou art blest or not,
 By reading the same lines?   O then come hither!
 And lay my book, thy head, and heart together."

EVERYONE who writes an autobiography
—perhaps everyone who keeps a diary—
must be an egoist. Certainly Bunyan was
an egoist. No one can read "Grace
Abounding" without feeling what an
immense interest he felt in himself. He
positively gloated over his sins; because
he had got rid of them. He piled up the
repetition of his miseries; because he felt
so happy in his new life. He remembered
all sorts of faults in others because they
had come into conflict with himself. He
recorded scores of trivial details because
they were part of the picture of himself
in which he delighted. Sometimes he is
almost like Rousseau in his disgusting
complacency, but then falls a rain of
penitential tears and blots out the picture.

The merit of " Grace Abounding to the Chief of Sinners " is that it is so entirely candid. At parts of it we are indignant with the vanity of the writer; but then, with a touch of nature, he contrives to make us his compassionate friends. As literature the book has a distinct place, but not a very high one. Its chief value is as an historical record, and for that purpose it has been continually quoted in the record of the writer's life. And almost everyone who reads it will find something in it which strikes home into his own life.

But it is surpassed as a record of contemporary manners by that most remarkable book " The Life and Death of Mr. Badman," which is a lurid record of lower-middle class life in the later years of Charles II. Bunyan knew all about the manners of such folk, those among them especially who haste to get rich, with no particular care for morals and only a tardy recognition of religion.

The book is written in the form of a dialogue between Mr. Wiseman, who tells the story and Mr. Attentive, who listens. A most grim and realistic study of sordid life it is; and I should advise anyone who wants to appreciate its full grimness or to make its grimness grimmer still to read it in the edition which has the "twelve compositions by George Woolliscroft Rhead and Louis Rhead designed to portray the deadly sins of the ungodly Mr. Badman's journey from this world to Hell."

Mr. Badman begins by being a bad boy, "notoriously infected with original corruption. . . . the ringleader and master-sinner from a child" among others, "the inventor of bad words and an example in bad actions." He served the devil betimes and a mighty liar he was, and a great pilferer from gardens and orchards: chickens (pullen) too would he snatch; all was fish that came to his net. Of course he abhorred Sunday, the Bible, sermons, prayer.

Sin, sin, and to do the thing that was
nought, that was what he delighted in, and
that from a little child. And then how he
swore : Bunyan seems to revel in telling
you. And how—Bunyan knew well that
this is the great temptation of countryfolk
—he swore at every beast he had to drive,
and most dreadful stories has Bunyan to
tell, out of his own knowledge, of men
whom the devil fetched because of their
apprenticeship in swearing, and their calling
him to their aid or to the discomfiture
of their foes or even their parents. To
young Badman, good masters made no
difference, good books were in vain : he
would only read " beastly romances and
books full of ribaldry "; and as for sermons
he would sleep through them, or look about
and giggle. Bad companions increased his
wickedness; bad women as well as bad men.
Bunyan sprinkles all the story with tales
from his own experience. Here is one of
them :

" When I was in prison, there came a woman to me that was under a great deal of trouble. So I asked her (she being a stranger to me) what she had to say to me. She said, she was afraid she should be damned. I asked her the cause of those fears. She told me, That she had some time since lived with a shopkeeper at Wellingborough, and had robbed his box in the shop several times of money, to the value of more than now I will say; and pray, says she, tell me what I shall do. I told her, I would have her go to her master, and make him satisfaction. She said, she was afraid; I asked her why? She said, she doubted he would hang her. I told her, that I would intercede for her life, and would make use of other friends too, to do the like; but she told me she durst not venture that. Well, said I, shall I send to your master, while you abide out of sight, and make your peace with him, before he sees you? and with that I asked her master's name. But all that she said in answer to this was, Pray let it alone till I come to you again. So away she went,

and neither told me her master's name nor
her own.   This is about ten or twelve years
since, and I never saw her again.   I tell you
this story, for this cause, to confirm your
fears, that such kind of servants too many
there be; and that God makes them sometimes like old Tod, of whom mention was
made before (through the terrors that he
lays upon them) to betray themselves." *

A worse tale illustrates the horrors of
uncleanness. It is that true tale which
Aubrey † tells of the wicked father, wild
Dayrell of Littlecote, who burnt the new-
born baby in the fire, and his bribe to
Popham, C.J. Bunyan, who was very
good at telling stories, improved it by a
number of veracious details. " This story,
the midwife's son, who was a minister,
told me."   Frightful indeed are the other
stories Bunyan tells : the whole atmosphere
of young Badman's life is one of filthiness
and disgust; and yet there is nothing in

* " The Life and Death of Mr. Badman," p. 42.
† " Brief Lives," ii. pp. 158–9.

it which Bunyan may not well have seen
and known. The story grows in horror
as we proceed, and there is nature in it
all: there are moments of success, alterna-
tions of something like satisfaction: good
influences striving with the sinner, yet all
rejected. Badman marries; and the poor
girl is at least a "professor": she has
children, one very gracious, three as bad as
their father, the rest not as bad as their
father nor as good as their mother. The
tale goes on to its inevitable end. The man
trades, and uses every kind of dishonesty.
He pretends to be good with the good, with
the bad he gives the reins to every evil
desire. He is as skilful as a modern swindler
in the management of bankruptcy: he is
adept in the manipulation of prices as
buyer and seller. He grows rich: he
delights in being praised and in praising
himself. God gives him a warning: he
breaks his leg one night when he is drunk.
And then there are many dreadful tales of

drunkards and of atheists : all, we may be sure, from the writer's own experience. Then when Badman becomes depressed the doctor assures him that the trouble is only physical. He repents. He sins again. His good wife dies. He marries a wicked one; and from her he suffers till at last he fails, for " his cups and his queans " have sapped his health : all his wealth was sinned away, and his wife and he in their wickedness are as poor as howlets. Then he came to death, quiet, deluded, with no sign of death-bed repentance. " I say there is no surer sign of a man's damnation than to die quietly after a sinful life, than to sin and die with a heart that cannot repent." Truly a dreadful end to a dreadful book.

Fearful as the story is, its fearfulness is doubled by the constant recurrence to facts of the writer's own knowledge : not always facts certainly, yet all such as Bunyan certainly believed to be true and not mere superstitions or fancies. And behind all it is an unmatched picture of the life of the class of men (if they were wicked) among whom the Bedford tinker lived.

In the " Holy War " Bunyan again shows his highest power. Its subject is the siege of Mansoul (the soul of man) by the forces of evil, with the alarums and excursions, the successes and set-backs which belong to such a fight. It is a very long tale, detailed in Bunyan's way, interspersed with many quips and happy sayings, many shrewd comments, many instances of intimate knowledge of human nature. Whether it would have been the best of English allegories if " The Pilgrim's Progress " had never been written, as Macaulay thinks, may be left where Froude left the question after contradicting Macaulay. It does not really matter. Certainly it is a very close allegory, vigorously and pungently written. But there is much special historical interest in it which is less prominent in

" The Pilgrim's Progress." Nothing is more remarkable about Bunyan, an extraordinarily alert and pertinacious personage, than that there should be so very little in his writings about contemporary politics. The Restoration, the oscillations between French and Dutch alliances, between Protestantism and Romanism, the Plague, the Fire, the Dutch in the Medway, the Court's corruption—all these things seem, save for a very few chance and dubious allusions, to leave him quite unmoved. Did he really care at all about his country, or only about his sect ?

A true answer would probably be that he cared only about the soul and God. That he saw God through a very narrow outlet, darkened by the niceties of a rigid theology, may partially account for this limitation. It may really be (though it is hard to believe it) that he set an example to Englishmen on starting for heaven alone. Yet no one can read " The Pilgrim's Progress "

without being sure that he saw many things
on the way. And in "The Holy War,"
perhaps, he saw more, and remembered
more of what he had seen before he began
his pilgrimage.

The country called Universe, says Bunyan,
is a beautiful one, and a fair and delicate
town is Mansoul. We are told of its walls
and palaces, of its King and its governors,
of Diabolus, the enemy, and his counsellors.
Of these last, Bunyan greatly enjoys himself in the descriptions : Mr. Will-be-will,
Mr. No-truth, Mr. Affection, Impudent,
Black-mouth, Hate-reproof, and so forth—
"like to like," quoth the devil to the
collier. These all married in the town
"and also begot and yielded many bad
brats, too many to be inserted." Through
such folk it was that Mansoul was easily
taken by Diabolus. And then came their
defence against the army of the king. Up
the tower over Ear-gate were the two great
guns, High-mind and Heady, cast by Mr.

Puff-up; but they did the King's men little harm, " though sometimes their shot would go by their ears with a Whizz."

As the fight goes against him, subtle are the arguments of Diabolus to Emmanuel, the King's son, to induce him to leave the town in his hands. Clear is the answer of the golden Prince : battle joined ; fierce fighting ; entrance forced ; streets cleared by slings ; the Recorder's house ; that old gentleman, Mr. Conscience; the brave exploits of Captain Execution. When the town is captured all comes right ; a general pardon : and Bunyan has a beautiful passage about the Prince's reception of the prisoners :

" Well, I told you before how the prisoners were entertained, by the noble Prince Emmanuel, and how they behaved them-selves before him, and how he sent them away to their homes, with pipe and tabor going before them. And now you must think that those of the town that had all this while waited to hear of their death, could not but be exercised with sadness of mind, and with thoughts that pricked like thorns. Nor could their thoughts be kept to any one point; the wind blew with them all this while at great uncertainties; yea, their hearts were like a balance that had been disquieted with a shaking hand. But, at last, as they with many a long look looked over the wall of Mansoul, they thought that they saw some returning to the town; and thought again, Who should they be too, who should they be! At last they discerned that they were the prisoners; but can you imagine how their hearts were surprised with wonder, especially when they perceived also in what equipage and with what honour they were sent home? They went down to the camp in black, but they came back to the town in white; they went down to the camp in ropes, they came back again in chains of gold; they went down to the camp with their feet in fetters, but came back with their steps enlarged under them; they went also to the camp looking for death, but they came back from thence with assurance of life; they went down to the camp with heavy hearts, but came back again with pipe and tabor playing before them. So, so soon as they were come to Eye-gate, the poor and tottering town of Mansoul adventured to give a shout, and they gave such a shout as made the captains in the prince's army leap at the sound thereof.

"Alas, for them, poor hearts! who could blame them since their dead friends were come to life again? for it was to them as life from the dead, to see the ancients of the town of Mansoul to shine in such splendour. They looked for nothing but the axe and the block; but behold! joy and gladness, comfort and consolation, and such melodious notes attending of them that was sufficient to make a sick man well." *

"The Holy War" is a remarkable and impressive book. There is no doubt at all that it represents a deep and genuine desire of the writer to show how dangerous

* "The Complete Works of John Bunyan," Vol. III. p. 48.

and difficult life is for every man, how the soul is beset on every side by temptations, how strong the devil is, yet how much stronger is God. That is at the bottom the whole lesson. But many interesting points emerge as we go through the book. There is nothing to show that Bunyan believed in instantaneous and irrevocable conversion of the soul to God. His experience, indeed, was all against it. Like Wesley, he knew the moral danger of a belief in man's security, however truly he may for the moment have accepted the love and pardon of God. There is through all the book, in Dr. Johnson's uncorrected phrase, a bottom of good sense. Though his purely theological tracts may often seem to protest against such a judgment, the writer of " The Holy War " was fundamentally sensible.

In this book, it must be admitted, his personages are not so vigorously alive as are the companions and foes of Pilgrim :

they are more often abstractions than personalities; and yet there are very often vivacious touches about them. The general judgment of mankind is still stern. Perhaps it represents what will always be the view of the man who, though " converted," is not fully educated. Mirth is inexorably banned. Bunyan would never have said with Milton, " Mirth, admit me of thy crew," or had even a sneaking kindness for " tipsy dance and jollity."

Sir Charles Firth has pointed out a conspicuous instance :

" ' Not guilty of pitilessness : all I did was to cheer up according to my name, for my name is not Pitiless but Cheer-up, and I could not abide to see Mansoul incline to melancholy.' But naturally this defence was useless and he was hanged like the rest. To Puritanism gaiety or merriment was suspicious : it suggested levity and savoured of sin, while a severe countenance and a stiff carriage connoted godliness. So it had been with the stricter sort of Puritans amongst the lower and middle classes throughout the early part of the 17th century, and so it was still when Bunyan wrote. The rigid suppression of many innocent amusements during the time of the Puritan triumph is paralleled by what happened in the city of Mansoul after its capture. Poor Harmless Mirth, on the pretext that his real name was Lasciviousness, was committed to prison, and so loaded with irons that he fell into a very deep consumption and died, while his two sons, Jolly and Griggish, were hanged straight off." *

On the other hand there is less animosity against Pope than in other books, if more against Pagan, if Pagan may be taken to represent the unbelief of Bunyan's time. Incredulity and Atheism have no mercy shown them.

Let me quote Sir Charles Firth again :

" ' The Doubters are such as have their

* *The Journal of English Studies*, Vol. I. p. 144.
Ω

name from their nature, as well as from the
lord and kingdom where they are born
their nature is to put a question upon every
one of the truths of Emmanuel, and their
country is called the land of Doubting, and
that land lieth far off and furthest remote
to the North, between the Land of Darkness
and the Valley of the Shadow of Death.
There were nine bands of these Doubters
in old Incredulity's army, the Election
Doubters, the Vocation Doubters, the
Grace Doubters, the Faith Doubters, the
Perseverance Doubters, the Resurrection
Doubters, the Salvation Doubters, the
Glory Doubters, and the Felicity Doubters
In the end they were beaten and destroyed
but once more old Incredulity got away
safely and raised a fresh army and came
back to renew the siege. He seems to
bear a charmed life. His kinsmen within
the city are killed too. Old Evil Question
ing who married Incredulity's niece, No
Hope, is executed, and most of their eight
children. The second of the eight children
survived to carry on the traditions of the
family. ' Mr. Unbelief was a nimble jack

him they could never lay hold of, though
they attempted to do it often.' " *

And that leads one to note Bunyan's
attitude towards the trial of prisoners in
this book. The proceeding is much the
same as in " The Pilgrim's Progress," and
it represents the writer's idea of the justice
of his time.   When the Diabolonians are
judged, we find that the Judge is on the
whole fair, but the jury are most violently
prejudiced.   Thus tells the historian of
Mansoul :

" Then, Mr. Belief, for he was the foreman, began.
" Gentlemen, quoth he, for the prisoners
at the bar, for my part I believe that they
all deserve death.   Very right, said Mr.
Trueheart, I am wholly of your opinion.
Nor do I at all question it, said Mr.
Heavenly-Mind.   When all such beasts as
these are cast out of Mansoul, what a goodly
town will it be then. . . . Then said the

* *The Journal of English Studies,* Vol. I. p. 146.

warm man and true hearted, Mr. Zeal-for-God, ' Cut them off.' "

The witnesses are (except that they are of Bunyan's mind) just as outrageous in their statements as those who bore witness against Christian. With the fullest desire to be on Bunyan's side, we cannot feel that he was fair to those who were not. We do not at all accept as just the adage, " Give a dog a bad name and hang him," and Bunyan almost tempts us now and then to go so far as to give the devil his due. Certainly he lived in a precarious day, and between the Romanists and the loose-livers of Charles's time he may well have feared to slip. He saw, too, another growing danger. Wars in Charles II's day were beginning to be made more for commerce than for religion. With infidelity there was also the rising commercialism. Great fortunes were being made. At many of the men of whom we learn from Pepys, and

Evelyn, and Aubrey's "Brief Lives," Bunyan may well have looked askance. Thus in the towns wealth was beginning to flaunt itself : simplicity was at a discount. Mansoul shows that clearly enough. More clearly still, as we have seen, is this sign of the times evidenced in " The Life and Death of Mr. Badman."

It is a long tale, capture, recapture, intrigue, detection, punishment, again and again, tedious to tell, but not at all, for his vivacity and distinctness, tedious to read. All through there are the same tell-tale names. Bunyan is determined you shall have no doubt who his personages are. They are black and white; he will have no whitey-brown, and young Diabolonians must be hung up, as certainly as older criminals, for their fathers' sakes as well as for their own. And so at last comes old Mr. Questioning to his death, because he had been " the receiver, the entertainer and the comforter of Doubters."

"Then stood forth Mr. Diligence, and said, 'My Lord, as I was upon my watch such a night, at the head of Bad Street, in this town, I chanced to hear a muttering within this gentleman's house; then thought I, what is to do here? So I went up close, but very softly, to the side of the house, to listen, thinking, as indeed it fell out, that there I might light upon some Diabolonian conventicle. So, as I said, I drew nearer and nearer, and when I was got up close to the wall, it was but a while before I perceived that there were outlandish men in the house; but I did well understand their speech, for I have been a traveller myself. Now hearing such language in such a tottering cottage as this old gentleman dwelt in, I clapt mine ear to a hole in the window, and there heard them talk as followeth. This old Mr. Questioning asked these Doubters what they were, whence they came, and what was their business in these parts? And they told him to all these questions, yet he did entertain them. He also asked what numbers there were of them, and they told him ten thousand men. He then asked them why they made no more manly assault upon Mansoul? And they told him; so he called their general coward for marching off when he should have fought for his Prince. Further, this old Evil-questioning wished, and I heard him wish, would all the ten thousand Doubters were now in Mansoul, and himself in the head of them. He bid them also to take heed and lie quat, for if they were taken they must die, although they had heads of gold.'" *

Bunyan ends his tale in his most truly spiritual way. He makes the Lord, Who welcomes back His lost ones, warn them of the dangers which still lie before them and appeal to them by the love that He has shown.

"O my Mansoul, I have lived, I have died; I live, and will die no more for thee. I live that thou mayest not die. Because I live thou shalt live also. I reconciled thee to my Father by the blood of my cross, and

* "Complete Works of John Bunyan," Vol. III. p. 103.

being reconciled thou shalt live through me. I will pray for thee, I will fight for thee, I will yet do thee good.

" Nothing can hurt thee but sin ; nothing can grieve me but sin; nothing can make thee base before thy foes but sin. Take heed of sin, my Mansoul.

" And dost thou know why I at first, and do still, suffer Diabolonians to dwell in thy walls, O Mansoul ? It is to keep thee wakening, to try thy love, to make thee watchful, and to cause thee yet to prize my noble captains, their soldiers, and my mercy.

" It is also that yet thou mayest be made to remember what a deplorable condition thou once wast in. I mean when, not some, but all did dwell, not in thy walls, but in thy castle, and in thy stronghold, O Mansoul !

" O my Mansoul, should I slay all them within, many there be without that would bring thee into bondage ; for were all those within cut off, those without would find thee sleeping, and then as in a moment they would swallow up my Mansoul. I therefore left them in thee, not to do thee hurt, the which they yet will, if thou hearken to them, and serve them; but to do thee good, the which they must, if thou watch and fight against them. Know, therefore, that whatever they shall tempt thee to, my design is that they should drive thee, not further off, but nearer to my Father, to learn thee war, to make petitioning desirable to thee, and to make thee little in thine own eyes." *

Two points remain which one should not forget. Bunyan had the chance to recall his own military experiences here. They may not have been very much, but they would serve. He had probably done little, if any, fighting in the open country, but he had taken part in a siege and been in great peril.

He had watched the training of troops too, and maybe become enamoured of it:

" O with what agility, nimbleness, dexterity, and bravery did these military men

* " Complete Works of John Bunyan," Vol. III. p. 107.

discover their skill in feats of war to the now
gazing town of Mansoul! They marched,
they counter-marched, they opened to the
right and left, they divided and sub-divided,
they closed, they wheeled, made good their
front and rear with their right and left
wings, and twenty things more, with that
aptness, and then were all as they were
again, that they took, yea, ravished the
hearts that were in Mansoul to behold it.
But add to this, the handling of their arms,
the managing of their weapons of war,
were marvellous taking to Mansoul and me.''

Yet he had not really studied the warfare
of his own day. What he tells of the attack
and defence of Mansoul are as much by
medieval as by modern models. He will
give his soldiers slings quite as often as
cannon. And perhaps what impressed him
most of all was the unconquerable deter-
mination of the officers to preach. In
Cromwell's army he had a great experience
of that. No doubt he had tried his hand at
the task himself and enjoyed it. So the
officers in the King's army must preach

against the Diabolonians as well as fight
them. But another touch is the domestic.
We know Bunyan loved his own little blind
girl. We see again and again how his heart
turned towards children. Even when he
paints one of his wicked women he cannot
help telling how she played with her child :

" I knew his father, his name was Mr.
Flatter, and his mother, before she was
married, was called by the name of Mrs.
Soothup ; and these two, when they came
together lived not long without this son,
and when he was born they called his name
Falsepeace. I was his playfellow, only I
was somewhat older than he ; and when
his mother did use to call him home from
his play, she used to say, ' Falsepeace,
Falsepeace, come home quick or I'll fetch
you.' Yea, I knew him when he was sucked ;
and though I was then but little, yet I can
remember that when his mother did use to
sit at the door with him, or did play with
him in her arms, she would call him twenty
times together, ' my little Falsepeace, my
pretty Falsepeace,' and ' O my sweet rogue

Falsepeace '; and again ' O my little bird Falsepeace '; and ' how do I love my child.' "

So we leave " The Holy War," and we cannot but feel that here, as in nearly all he wrote, Bunyan has been telling us about himself. He may have taken for his own motto the lines of Wither :

> " Give me that heart which in itself doth war
> With many frailties (who like traitors are,
> In some besieged fort), and hath to do
> With outward foes and inward terrors too,
> Yet of himself and them a conquest makes,
> And still proceeds in what he undertakes."

These are Bunyan's great books ; yet all the while that he was writing them, he was preaching and writing converting and controversial theology. Much of this—though after all not so very long ago—has gone on to the dust-heap.

Says the editor of Bunyan's works in 1862, Mr. Henry Stebbing—" The works of

Bunyan constitute a library of practical divinity. With the exception of Baxter, no writer has treated of so large a variety of topics, or illustrated Christian doctrine in language at once so forcible and simple." This is a bold claim : rash, most readers to-day will think. The distaste with which many of his writings will be read (if ever they are to-day) is due to two causes : his almost unique *cacoëthes scribendi*, and the virulence with which his pen set down the sharp words he used in controversy, such as his public disputation in Bedford with the Quaker Burroughs, whose views he most unfairly distorts. But polemics were a part of Bunyan's life which cannot be ignored if we are to understand him. It will be well, therefore, briefly to survey what may be called his purely theological writings.

This, at least, may be said of them all. They are very clear : there is no doubt as to what the writer means, as to his theological doctrine or his practical advice.

Early in his career comes : " Some Gospel truths opened, according to the Scriptures." It is an attack upon the Quakers, whose teaching he, like most of his contemporaries, did not fully understand. If Cromwell, who had some traces at least of a liberal mind, should not comprehend them, how should Bunyan ? Sometimes one is not clear that they always understood themselves. In this tract he was determined to assert the Lord's real divinity and humanity, and to appeal to his readers through His incarnation—" Therefore, I say unto thee, in the Name of the Lord Jesus, the Son of Mary, the Son of God, the very creator of heaven and earth, and all things that are therein, have a care for thyself, for the devil doth watch for thee day and night." So he sets forth the orthodox creed : and adds " some questions to the Quakers." What he said was disputed : so he writes again a " Vindication . . . according to the Scriptures," an answer to Edward Burroughs. This has the characteristic of all his writings—a repeated use of texts, relevant and sometimes irrelevant to his arguments. All his theology comes from the Bible, so far as he understands it. It begins the long series of popular Protestant tracts which lasted in its full vigour at least till the time of John Charles Ryle, Bishop of Liverpool. They are largely sermons that have been preached and now are printed; as sermons, missing some of their effect because they are so largely addressed to people who do not go to church and hear them; as tracts, trenchant and coming home to all who will read them.

Of these, then, we have a typical example in "Sighs from Hell or the Groans of a Damned Soul," an explication of the parable of Dives and Lazarus, very stark and stern. This was introduced by a letter from John Gifford, in the same style, but hardly with Bunyan's lucid directness. Now came the little touches which must have made

the preacher so interesting to listen to.
The dogs " will not be beguiled " : they
must have the scraps.   Men's fondness for
dogs.   Some cannot go half a mile from
their home without a dog at their heels,
yet they will very willingly go half a score
without the company of a Christian.   But
how long the sermon is !   The preacher
must have turned the hour-glass indeed.
The passion for length grew upon him.   He
was never content without explaining every
text he came across, nor would he use one
word where two would do.

So again with " The Doctrine of the Law
and Grace unfolded."   Here comes out
the bitterest Predestinarianism :

" The faithfulness of God calls for irre-
coverable ruin to be poured out on those
that shall live and die under this covenant.
If thou having sinned but one sin against
this covenant, and shouldst afterwards
escape damning, God must be unfaithful
to himself and his word ; which both agree

as one. First, he would be unfaithful to himself; to himself, that is, to his justice, holiness, righteousness, wisdom and power, if he should offer to stop the runnings out of his justice, for the damning of them that have offended it. And, secondly, he would be unfaithful to his word, his written word." *

When we hear of Bunyan's tolerance, we must remember that it never allowed him to believe that there were not many whom God had covenanted to damn, though here it is true that it is " under the law." " The Doctrine of the Law and Grace unfolded " extends to nearly a hundred large octavo pages, double columns. After this a much simpler and more beautiful discourse concerning prayer. It has a really admirable definition :

" For the first, *what prayer is*. Prayer is a sincere, sensible, affectionate outpour-

* " Doctrine of the Law and Grace," Works, Vol. I. p. 191.

R

ing of the heart or soul to God, through Christ, in the strength and assistance of the Holy Spirit, for such things as God hath promised, or according to the word, for the good of the church, with submission, in faith, to the will of God." *

These all are early writings or sermons. Then came the time when Bunyan began to preach in the prison; where indeed there was large " liberty of prophesying." It is not to be imagined that the gaolers of Charles II's day were harsh to those who were confined *causa religionis* : such met and prayed and preached quite freely. Bunyan says :

" Upon a certain first-day, I being together with my brethren in our prison-chamber, they expected that, according to our custom, something should be spoken out of the word for our mutual edification ; but at that time I felt myself, it being my

* " The Complete Works of John Bunyan," Vol. I. p. 262.

turn to speak, so empty, spiritless, and barren, that I thought I should not have been able to speak among them so much as five words of truth with life and evidence ; but at last it so fell out that providentially I cast mine eye upon the eleventh verse of the one and twentieth chapter of this prophecy."

And it is from this that there comes that exposition of " The Holy City or the New Jerusalem." As published it begins with some pungent letters—one to " the mother of harlots," the Church of Rome. Out of its very lengthy lucubrations it may be discovered that Bunyan had little if any thought of an organised Church or of a form of admission thereto : and those only should be admitted who " are visible saints by calling." This again is about eighty double-columned pages. A sermon on the Resurrection of the Dead and Eternal Judgment is slightly shorter : a curious detailed exposition, in which

Bunyan is sure that as he " said concerning things that are candied, that this body when it is risen shall lose all that sourness and stink that now by reason of sin and infirmity cleaveth to it; neither shall its lumpishness or unwieldiness be any impediment to it acting after the manner of angels." Then " Justification an Imputed Righteousness " is one of those curious pieces of non-natural interpretation in which the seventeenth century delighted, but with much of the writer's sound practical advice interspersed. " A confession of my faith " shows the limits of his tolerance and willingness for church fellowship. " A reason of my practice in worship " shows the nature, not too violent, of his acceptance of the Baptist opinions. Baptism he regards as admission to a particular (apparently a local) church, for the visible church is a particular church, " the universal being utterly invisible and known to none but God "; yet, as the next treatise

in his Works shows, he regarded " differences
in judgment about water baptism " as
" no bar to communion." In this he is
partly controversial—in a controversy long
dead, with persons quite forgotten—partly
assertive of an entire emancipation from
the old and continuous doctrine of the
Church. On the other hand his " Instructions for the Ignorant " is quite a reasonable
catechism, so far as it goes, failing only
through omissions. Among sermons again
is " Saved by Grace, or a discourse on
the Grace of God "; and " Christian behaviour " (full of sound common-sense) ;
" Come and welcome to Jesus Christ," on
S. John vi. 37 (verbose and of course
quite unsacramental) ; "The barren fig-tree,"
full of grim descriptions of sickness and
death, which may be compared with
" Seasonable counsel, or, advice to suf-
ferers," written in 1684, which has much
real feeling in it and much sound advice.
Other sermons have little, if anything,

that is of special note in them : " The
Pharisee and the Publican," a very long
sermon indeed ; " The Strait Gate," a
treatise on the fear of God ; " The Jerusalem sinner saved, or, good news for the
vilest of men " ; " Israel's hope encouraged."
To these are added some notes, found after
the writer's death, which are no more,
clearly, than sketches for sermons " of the
Trinity and a Christian " and " of the
Law and a Christian " ; " Light for them
that sit in darkness," very clearly setting
forth the Eternity of the Son of God,
the delight of the Father : " While as yet
he had not made the earth or the fields, or
the highest part of the dust of the world,
all things were made by him and without
him was not anything made that was made,
and he is before all things and by him
all things consist." Here he begins well,
but he goes on so long that he becomes
befogged in his theology, and his readers
can hardly be anything else. " The great-

ness of the soul " has some fine thoughts
in it, finely expressed, but some curious
quibblings about (for example) the " lowest
hell "—degrees of glory in heaven, degrees
of torment in hell. Bunyan in all these
sermons suffers from the penalty of a bitter
literalness dependent upon nothing beyond
the Authorised Version. So " Solomon's
temple spiritualized " is really best taken
in its author's own words—" I dare not
presume to say that I know I have hit
right in everything, but this I can say,
I have endeavoured so to do. True, I
have not for these things fished in other
men's waters : my Bible and Concordance
are my only library in my writings. Wherefore, courteous reader, if thou findest anything, either in word or matter, that thou
shalt judge doth vary from God's truth,
let it be counted no man's else but mine ;
pray God also to pardon my fault. Do
thou also lovingly pass it by and receive
what thou findest will do thee good."

Nothing could be more timely than this when we read a treatise so full of confused theology, often verging on savagery, in regard to the doctrine of election and reprobation, leading to the awful conclusion that " it is not in every one's will and power to be saved."

How different is the next sermon, on " A Holy Life, the Beauty of Christianity," or that on " The Excellency of a broken heart," one of the very last things written. When Bunyan turned to commentary-making, as in " An Exposition of the first ten chapters of Genesis," it is natural that he should be less successful : nor really can much praise be given to the Exposition of 2 Tim. iv. 6–8. " The righteous man's desires " and " Christ a complete Saviour " say little or nothing that Bunyan has not often said before. There are several more sermons, which fill nearly a whole large volume; but little is there to be remembered in them, save here and there such a sad outlook on the

decay of goodness as good men in their last
years often take. Controversy comes forward again. There are the long tirades
against the orthodox Fowler, and Penn
the Quaker. So on and on through many
double-paged columns of exposition and
exhortation.

For the most part we have avoided reference to Bunyan's controversies, of which
those with Fowler (the Church of England)
and Burroughs (the Society of Friends) are
the most prominent, because in neither case
would sympathy now be with Bunyan, and
the subjects of contention are moribund,
if not quite dead. Really, patience gives
out at last, and we put away the rest of the
tracts we have read and say nothing about
them. Then his last sermon, preached
in July 1688. All these are best passed
by, that we may be content with the words
quoted : let us choose only what will do
us good. We may turn away from the
arid pages to words, preached at the end,
which show Bunyan almost at his best.

" The broken heart is hard to bear, for soul-pain is the sorest pain. With such a man God has wrestled and given him a fall, and now he crouches and cringes and craves for mercy. Like one with a broken limb who so far from hectoring it with a man is afraid lest even a child should touch him, so he begs of God to deal with him with tender hands. Once being at an honest woman's house, I after some pause, asked her how she did; very badly, was her reply—I am afraid I shall not be saved. Breaking out with heavy heart she said, ' Ah Goodman Bunyan! Christ and a pitcher; if I had Christ though I went and begged my bread with a pitcher, it would be better with me than I think it is now.' This woman had her heart broken, she wanted Christ. This cry of Christ and a pitcher made a melodious noise in the ears of the very angels. At first our pride is laid low. If a man be proud of his strength or manhood, a broken leg will maul him; and if a man be proud of his goodness a broken heart will maul him. Yet a broken heart or a contrite spirit is a heaven-sent blessing."

We certainly end the prose nobly. Bunyan tried also to be a poet. He had not been in prison a year when he put out his " Profitable Meditations." Later came " Meditations on the Four Last Things," and " Ebal and Gerizim " (1664) and " Prison Meditations " (1665). For the sake of poetry no one would read any of these; but in the last occur the famous lines, imitative of Lovelace :—

> " For though men keep my outward man
>   Within their locks and bars,
>   Yet by the faith of Christ I can
>   Mount higher than the stars."

None of these show the brightness of the verses interspersed in " The Pilgrim's Progress," but the lines quoted show that the writer had memories of other poets, as when he wrote,

> " Who would true valour see
>   Let him come hither !
> One here will constant be,
>   Come wind, come weather."

As a writer of verse Bunyan must be ranked

among those whom injudicious patronage
has often pushed to the front, from the
Farmer's Boy to the egregious poet Close.
Perhaps in all English literature only one
has forced his own way by genius, Burns;
only one deserved to be produced by
patronage, John Clare; only one has been
able by a combination of both to assume,
in his own life-time, a place secure in
letters, Patrick McGill. Beside these
Bunyan has no place at all. Certainly he
has sparks of talent, but not poetic talent,
only a sort of natural childish vivacity.
Of that not a few instances could be given
if it were worth while. In his more solemn
metres he becomes as tedious as does Burns.
More commonly he is too apt to sink to
such doggerel as of " Man by nature " :

> " From God he's a backslider,
>   Of ways he loves the wider;
>   With wickedness a sider,
>   More venom than a spider.
>   In sin he's a confider,
>   A make-hate and divider;
>   Blind reason is his guider,
>   The devil is his rider."

The " Divine Emblems "—its full title
is " Divine Emblems : or Temporal Things
Spiritualized; calculated for the use of
Young People "—is an early attempt to
produce spiritual laws from the natural
world. It led up to Mrs. Turner's
" Cautionary Stories " as well as to much
tedious poetry from Watts. As Mr. F. J. H.
Darton has put it, Bunyan's poetry is bad,
but his morality is sound. This is Bunyan's
aim :

" I do't to show them how each fingle-fangle
  On which they doting are, their souls entangle,
As with a web, a trap, a gin, a snare,
  And will destroy them, have they not a care."

And this is an example of his method of
teaching :

ON THE CACKLING OF A HEN
" The Hen, so soon as she an egg doth lay,
  Spreads the fame of her doing what she may :
  About the yard a-cackling she doth go,
  To tell what 'twas she at her nest did do.
  Just thus it is with some professing men
  If they do ought that's good; they, like our hen,
  Cannot but cackle out where e'er they go.
  And what their right hand does, their left must
    know."

Let us add to Bunyan some references to practical matters : for what is a hymn if it is not sung ?   Now who ever gave better advice on this than John Wesley ?   Here it is :

1. Learn the tunes.

2. Sing them as printed.

3. Sing all.   " If it is a cross to you, take it up and you will find a Blessing."

4. Sing lustily and with a good courage.

5. Sing modestly.   Do not bawl.

6. Sing in time.   Do not run before or stay behind.

7. Above all, sing spiritually.   Have an eye to God in every word you sing.

Could or would Bunyan do this ?   One wonders.   Bunyan at least did not write the " Busy Bee " which no one can be imagined as attempting to sing.

The " Divine Emblems " is known to most readers of Bunyan.   It turned out, on the discovery of a small quarto volume

in 1886, to be simply a reduced version
of the " Book for Boys and Girls; or
Country Rhymes for Children by J.B.,"
published in 1686, a collection of verses for
children prefaced by a kind of reproduc-
tion of the old horn-book then becoming
obsolete. It was reprinted in facsimile in
1889 with a delightful introduction by
Dr. Brown. It is well worth looking
through if only because it shows a real
love and understanding of children, a true
man's real humanity. Froude admired the
lines on a swallow, but the verses are marred
to modern eyes by the question whether
a bird could fly if she had no wings, irre-
sistibly suggesting Chadband and Snagsby.
To know Bunyan we must read all he wrote.
But gladly we forget much of it.

He was no faultless writer, but certainly
he remains among the glories of English
seventeenth-century literature. We could
not put him with Quarles or Crashaw or
George Herbert, and we cannot but feel

that Milton would look—perhaps did look
—upon him askance, not only because
they represented two quite different types
of Puritanism, but also because the loose
writing of the peasant would make the
learned purist shudder. But, strange as it
may seem, there is something more than
chronology which links Bunyan to Shakespeare as well as to Defoe. It is his deep
knowledge of the ways and mind of man.

THERE is no doubt at all what Bunyan looked like : he was a more than famous enough man for artists to desire to paint him. The best, or at any rate a most life-like, portrait is in the National Portrait Gallery, by T. Sadler. It shows a fat, some-what heavy, countenance, with long, rather greasy, hair, bright eyes with possibly a slight cast, a light moustache, a good strong heavy hand holding a book : alto-gether a stalwart, good-humoured-looking man, such as one often sees still among those who have served in the army and settled down to a comfortable way of life. A good honest fellow, we say, as we look at his portraits : and yet is there not something a little like a cast in his eye ?

Was there a cast in his theology? He was brought up a Church of England man. His father followed the Church till he died. Fundamentally Bunyan learnt her theology, but then, when he began to read the Bible for himself, he went off, as so many of his time did, into curious interpretations. The army preachers may have been the first men who caused him seriously to think of religion. There was every variety to be had among the Parliament's forces. The Presbyterians there soon had to make way for the Independents. Baillie, coming from Scotland, was horrified. " We all conceive," he wrote, " that our silly simple lads are in great danger of being infected by their company, and if that pest enter in our army, we fear it may spread." But there was no religious liberty in the army : among the many inventions which the reading of the Bible by ignorant men produced, there were errors regarded as " intolerable " as well as views which were tolerated.* Bunyan when he became a preacher may well have looked round for a Body of Divinity. He found it partly in his chilhood's faith and his parish priest's instructions, partly in the systems of Calvin and Luther which men talked so much of, partly in the beliefs of the friends he loved. So he became a very free Baptist.

When we ask how Bunyan stands towards the body to which he belonged, in its theology to-day, no better answer can be given than that very kindly given me by Dr. Whitley, the learned Secretary and Editor of the Baptist Historical Society.

" There were two sides to Bunyan, each of which is well represented in one or other of two modern Baptist groups.

" Ecclesiastically, he stood all but alone, determined to hold fellowship ' with saints as saints,' irrespective of their precise

* See Sir C. Firth, " Cromwell's Army," chapter xiii.

affiliation. To that position I imagine the
great majority of the churches in the
Baptist Union have come, so that members
worship naturally in any Free Church
to-day if no Baptist church is available.
And Baptist ministers occasionally accept
invitations to the pastorates of other
bodies, as is shown with Dr. Norwood,
Dr. Meyer, Mr. Campbell Morgan, Dr. Aked
and others in America. But American
Baptists are by no means of this type,
and even here, a minister who goes to
another communion is viewed somewhat
askance.

" Theologically, he was quite Calvinist.
And there is still a large group of Baptist
churches which adheres to the Westminster
Confession (with Baptist modifications).
These, however, are not only ' Particular '
in their conception of Redemption, but also
' Strict ' in their limits of communion, in
that respect quite contrary to Bunyan.
These churches have a very high standard
of piety, but they are hardly organized,
and on principle can hardly aim at conversion, as they are far less known than

their numbers might suggest. ' Ebenezer '
at Basingstoke, and ' Salem ' at Ports-
mouth, do preserve much of Bunyan's
intense Calvinistic theology, devoid probably of his passion for evangelization." *

And I would quote also an eminent Presbyterian, yet remembering that Bunyan would
not join any Presbyterian body :

" I don't think I can say more than that
John Bunyan's Theology was Theology
of the 17th century, and even Baptists
to-day live in the 20th. Seventeenth-
century Theological categories are those
of no brand of the Protestant churches
to-day, except in small and obscurantist
sections of them." †

Anyhow Bunyan's place is certainly
among " dissenters."

So it comes that, from among the leaders
in English religion—yet perhaps " guides "
is the better word—it is tempting to pick

* Letter from Dr. Whitley to W. H. Hutton,
Oct. 12, 1927.

† Letter from Dr. Carnegie Simpson to W. H. H.
Oct. 4, 1924.

out, for comparison, or contrast, John
Bunyan and John Wesley.

The one breathes always the open air,
though so much of his life is passed in
prison : he seems to write with difficulty :
he never quite shakes off the feeling of the
uneducated that what is in print must be
true. So there is a great contention within
him. He loves the open air, he delights
in mountain and rivers : he treats life
always as an ascent and progress as a
battling with the waters. What men have
written confuses him : he wastes innumer-
able hours in trying to understand it or
confute it. Naturally he sees everything,
and artificially he puzzles over everything.
Yet always he is open, uncontrolled : he is
the natural naked man, though he must
struggle with the shackles of dogma and
stir wearily in the clothes of convention.
Wesley is very different. He never quite
shakes off the pedant, the college don.
Hardly ever will he accept what other

people say. He must always criticise : he even comes near sometimes to a criticism of the Bible. The world is his parish, and he goes about with as little apparent reluctance among countesses as among colliers. But he has the masterful spirit of the dominie : under all his love for humanity he is at heart a pedant. Bunyan feels himself always the equal of men and women. Wesley feels himself their superior. Wesley cries aloud for mercy on the sins of others. Bunyan weeps tears of blood for his own. With all his astounding service to mankind, Wesley is always a conceited egoist : but Bunyan is a frail man among human sinners. The one reaches to spiritual heights beyond the other, whose lot it has been to sound the depths, a common man among common men. So Bunyan could never have led a crusade or founded a new sect or organised a religious victory. Yet he understood men and women as Wesley never did : and most of all children.

The conspicuous virtue which Wesley lacked was that which almost every religious leader from Christ Himself and onwards has displayed, a love of children. How strangely differs the hideous discipline of Kingswood school from " Suffer the little children to come unto Me." How near to the divine words are Bunyan's child verses, his love of babies' toys and games. Wesley's courage is bred of stern discipline : but it is out of weakness that Bunyan was made strong. The former belongs to the class about whom there are almost too many biographical details, the latter to those for whom we have too few. And, for that very reason perhaps, Bunyan was a man about whom, especially if the facts of his life and character are not well known, it is easy to write a great deal of imaginative nonsense. It is also easy to paint an inspiring picture of him, preaching to thousands who hang on his words, bringing healing to souls that suffer. But likewise it would not be difficult to describe him as a hard-hearted bigot. There is a story, probably as apocryphal as that the last words heard by Louis XVI were " Son of S. Louis ascend to heaven," that a Bishop in the Albigensian Crusade urged on the soldiers by saying " Kill them all, God will know His own." When one reads the trials of the bad folk in " The Holy War," still more when one reads the bitterest of Bunyan's polemical tracts, one is tempted to believe that he would have given the same order, or, if not " because God will know," because John Bunyan knew who were not God's own and how some were damned whatsoever they might do. Bunyan so often dreams of a merciless God that one wonders if he were merciless himself. Yet one is sure that, through his savage Calvinism, gentleness was always breaking in. His was a much sweeter soul than his theology, when he listened to it, would allow. His mind was in water-tight compartments. The bitter dogmatist slinks into the background when the lover of children, the lover of scenes and characters beautiful to behold, comes before our eyes. The man who hated Pope and Pagan and Quakers and an Apostolic ministry was the man whose eyes beheld the Delectable Mountains and whose soul kindled when Mr. Greatheart flashed his sword. It is by that side of his nature that we remember him, and then we love him. He went back from the cruelties and crudities of the Civil War to mend his pots and pans, says Sir Charles Firth. Most true : he was a coarse and common man. But also he went forward to the Cross, where his burden fell from his shoulders, and he passed onwards to the love of God and the love of man. Bunyan judged others very harshly, yet we cannot judge him so. As we close " The Pilgrim's Progress " we lay a laurel wreath upon his grave.

THE END

Index

Index